CRUISING

BY FRANCO DUPUY

DIARIES

CRUISING IS ANONYMOUS

CRUISING IS FURTIVE

CRUISING IS DARK

CRUISING IS SILENT

CRUISING IS FREE

CRUISING IS RISKY

A Set Margins' publication

BY FRANCO DUPUY

Oh, the night is my world
City light painted girl
In the day nothing matters
Its the night time that flatters

Self Control
Laura Branigan

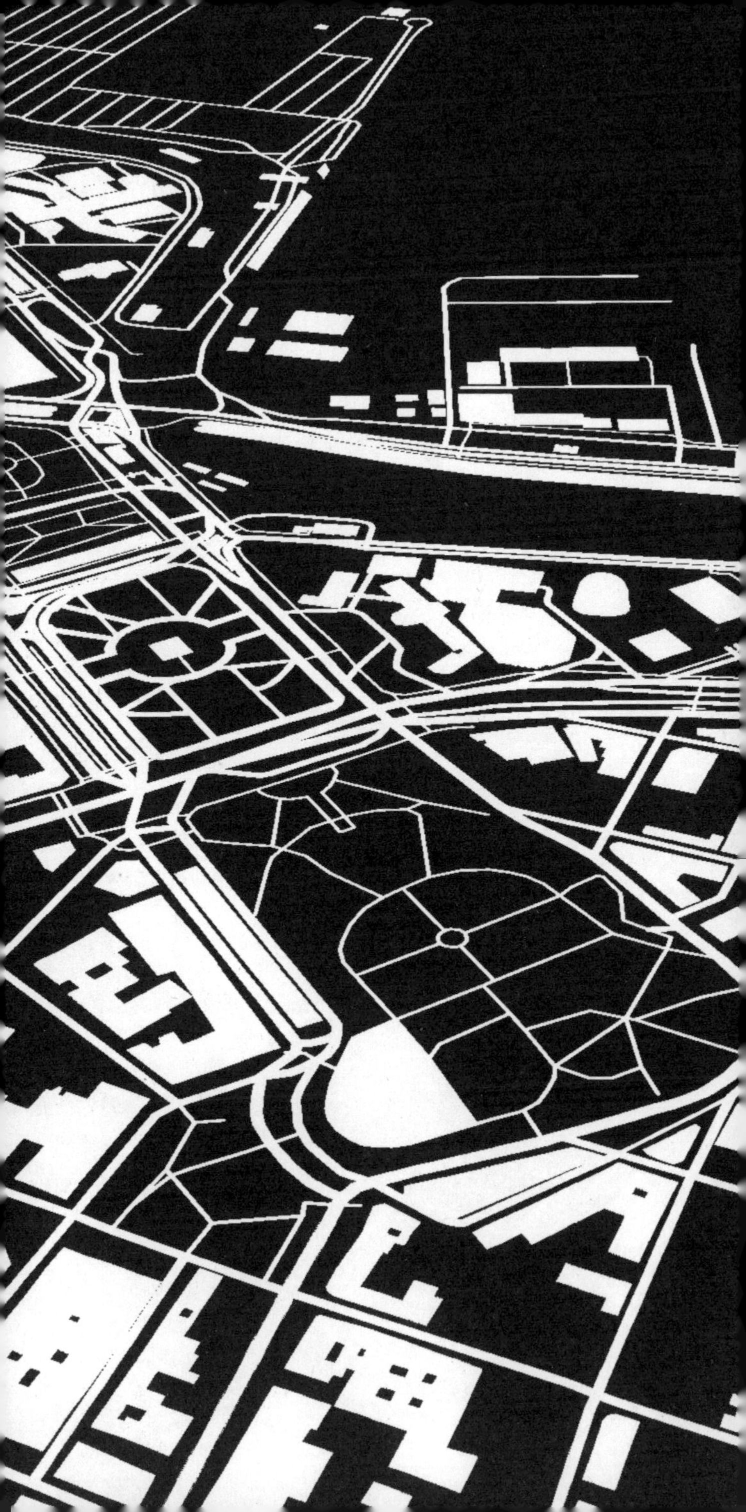

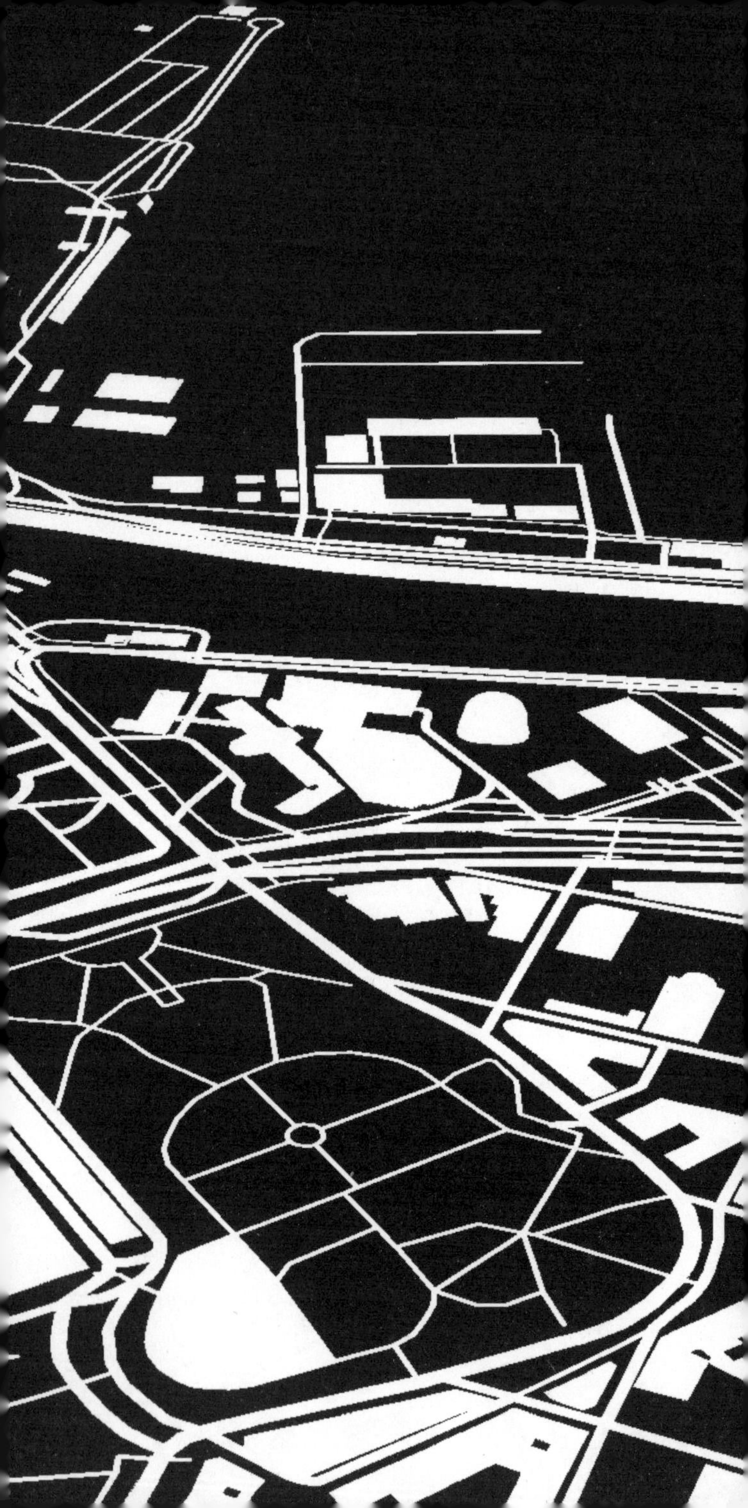

01. Heras Park

02. Park's Public Restrooms

03. Odyssey Theatre

01. Heras Park

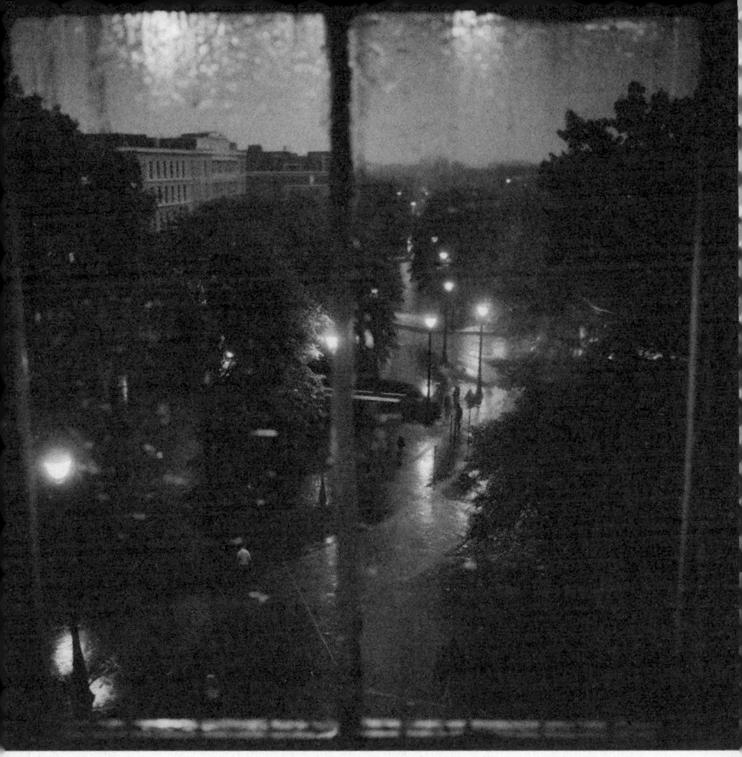

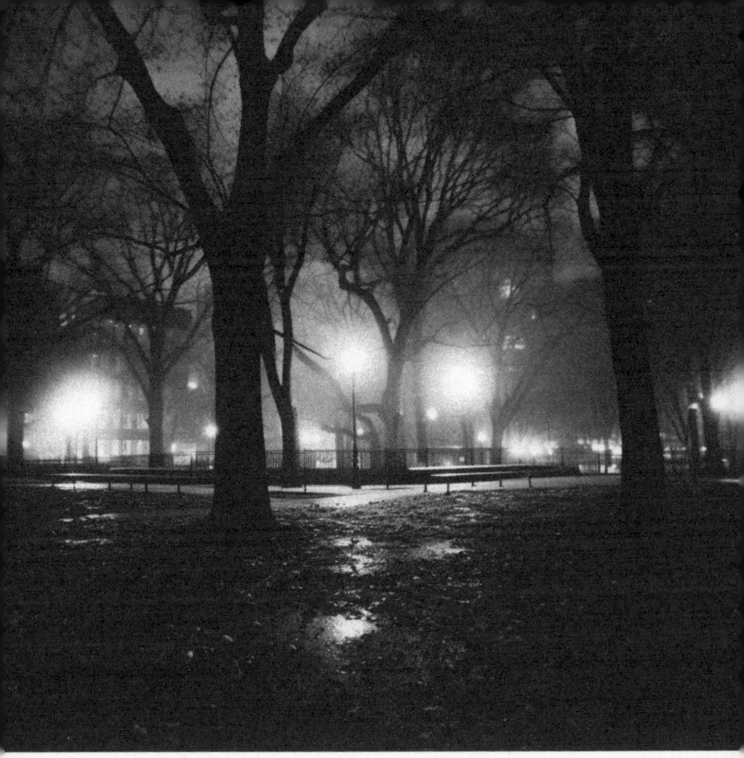

The new streetlights make cruising a bit harder, but some nights they're off in certain areas (dont know why, it's really random).

A bit risky at dawn, but if you stay alert, it's all good.

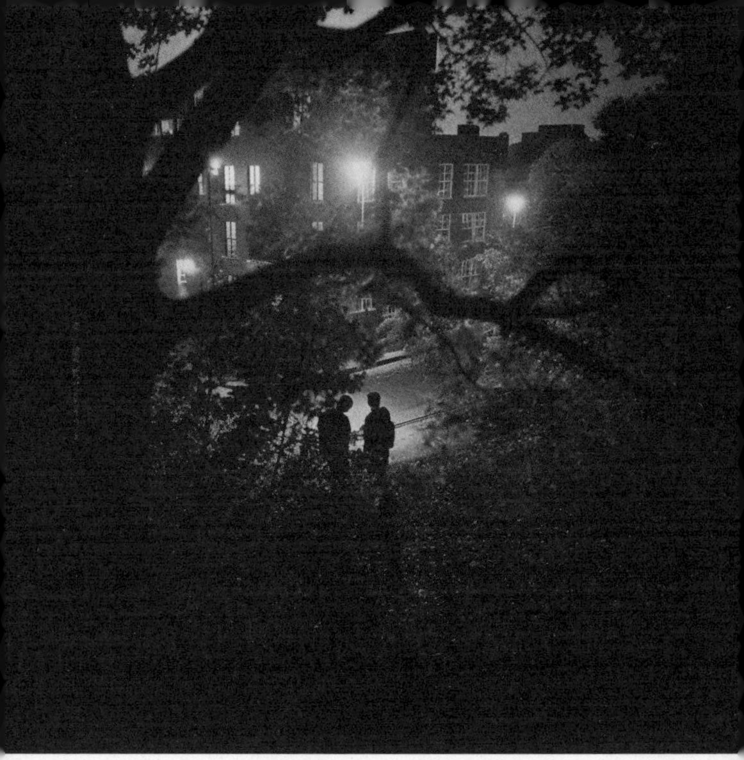

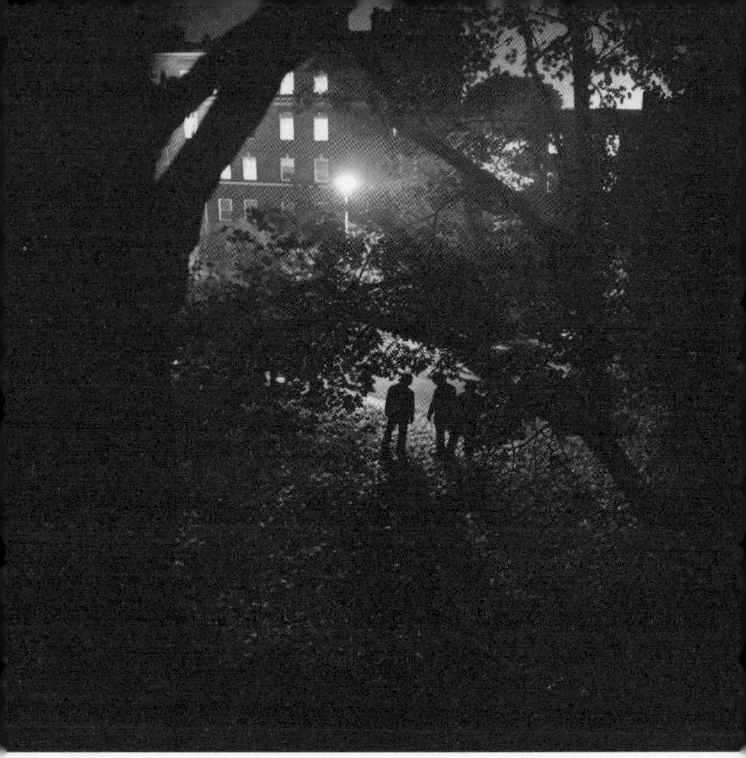

On weekdays, it's prime if you're in the area to check out the renowned park bathrooms.

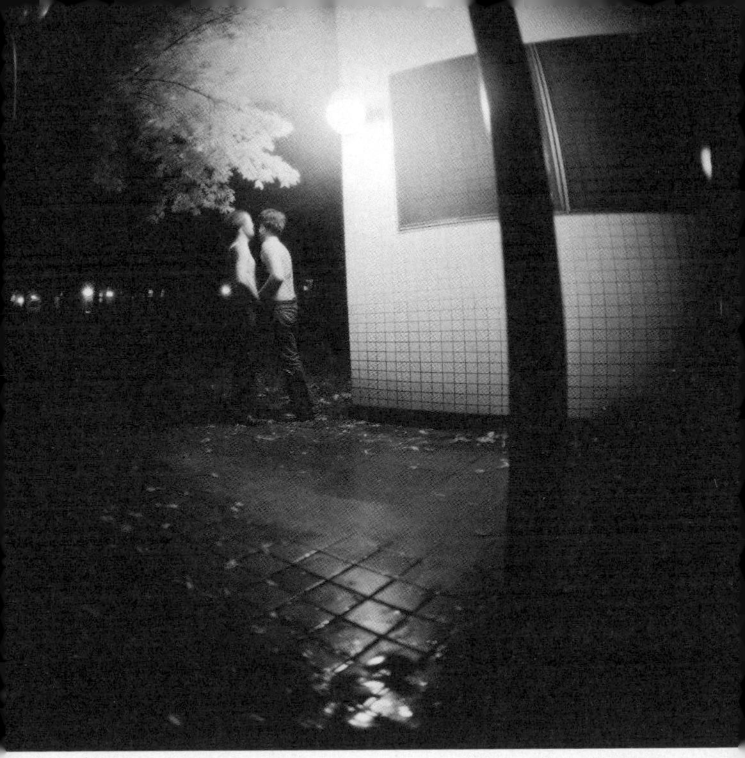

I call it 'The Mating Dance'.

Once you lock eyes, the dance begins—not just to gauge interest, but to scout the next hookup spot.

This walking/dancing technique is key for any encounter. It's crucial to make sure the vibe feels mutual and not like harassment or worse.

You look at him, and you walk.
You turn back to look again.
That's the 'follow me' signal.

The pace needs to be slow. Slowing down is a good sign. The message is pretty easy to get.

Either one can bail on the dance at any moment, nothing personal.

02. Park's Public Restrooms

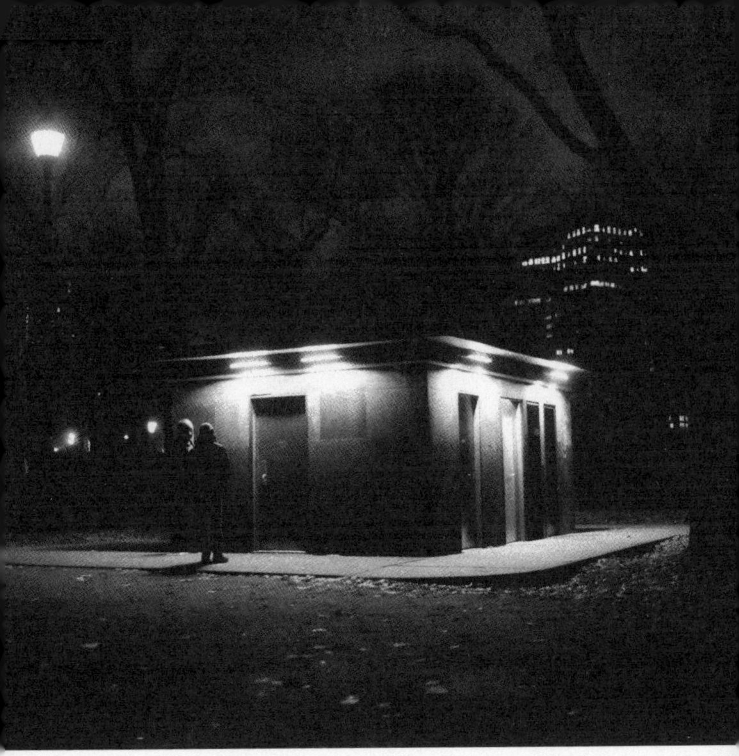

From the central fountain,
head towards the south
exit.
150 meters down, you'll
spot them -

By then, you're far enough
from the crowd

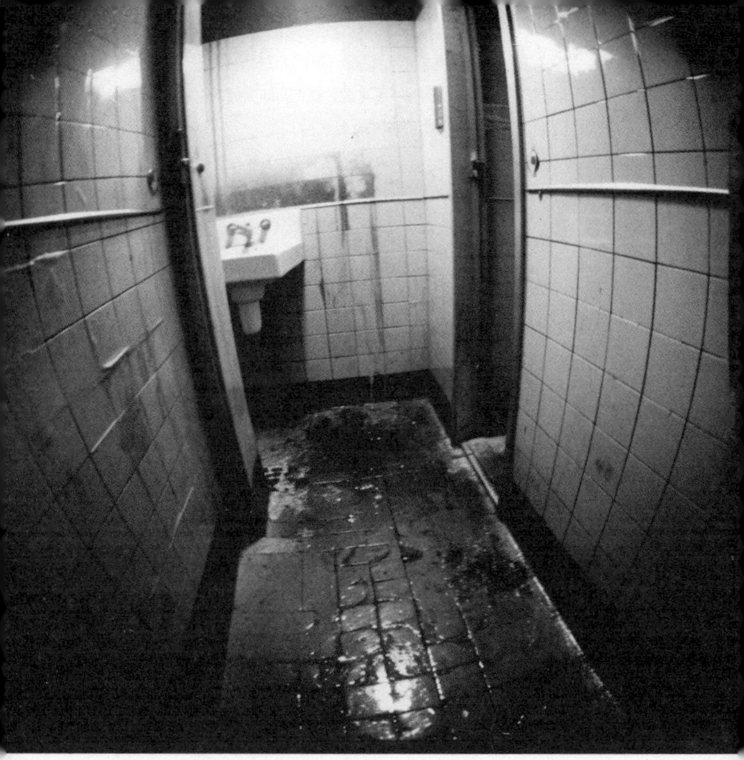

There's always someone smoking at the door. If you go in and the guy outside follows you, there's not much left to figure out.

Smoking is a noble habit.

The stalls are small, but the doors go all the way to the floor, fitting you both.

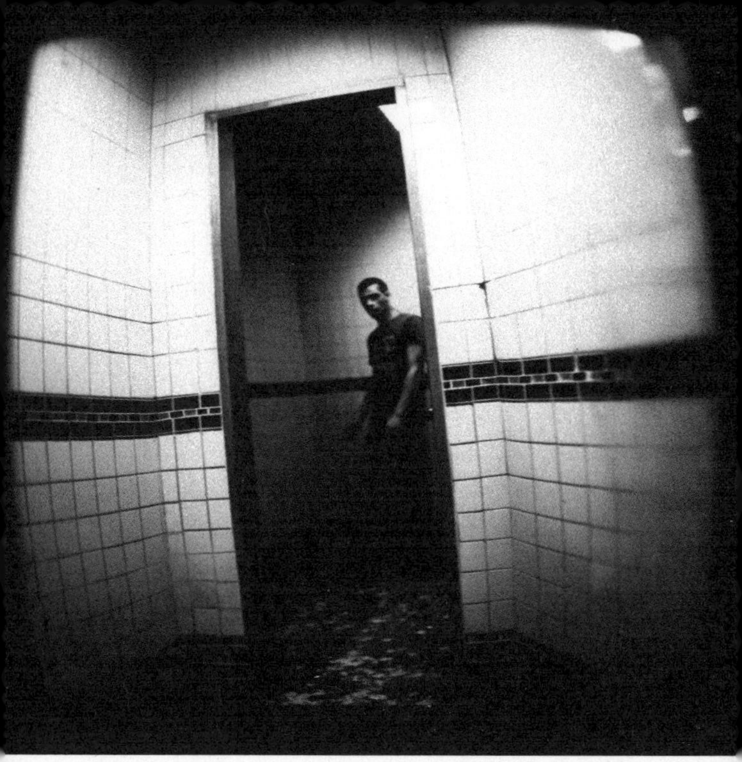

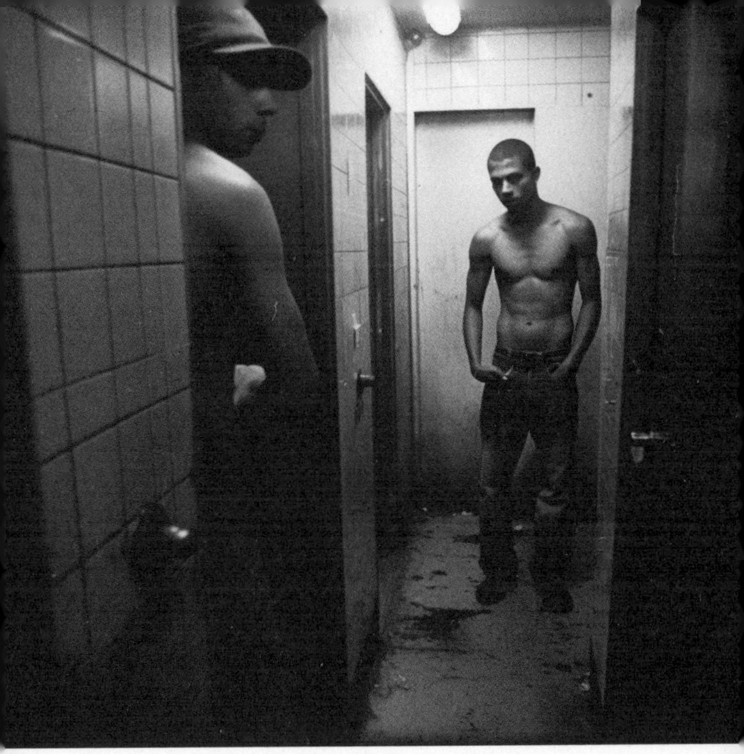

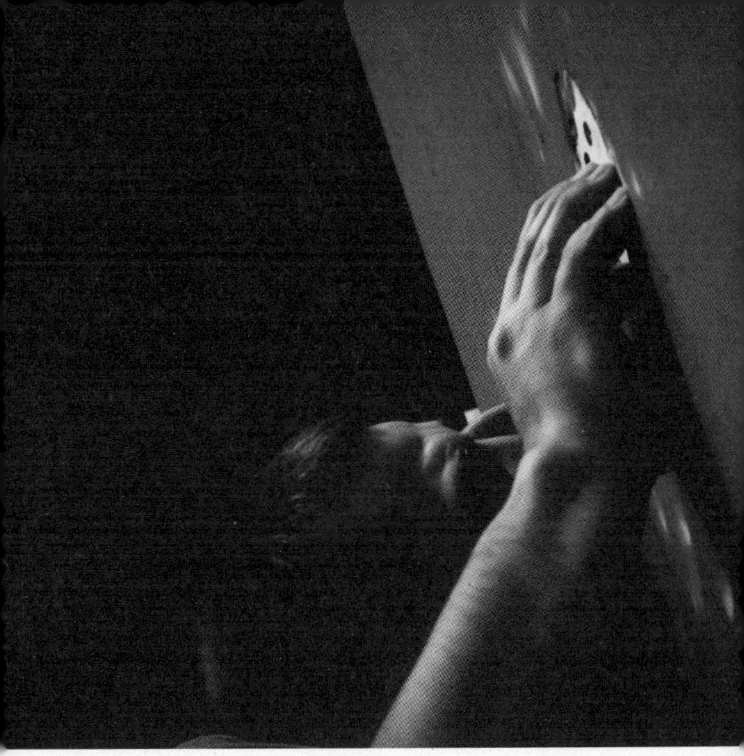

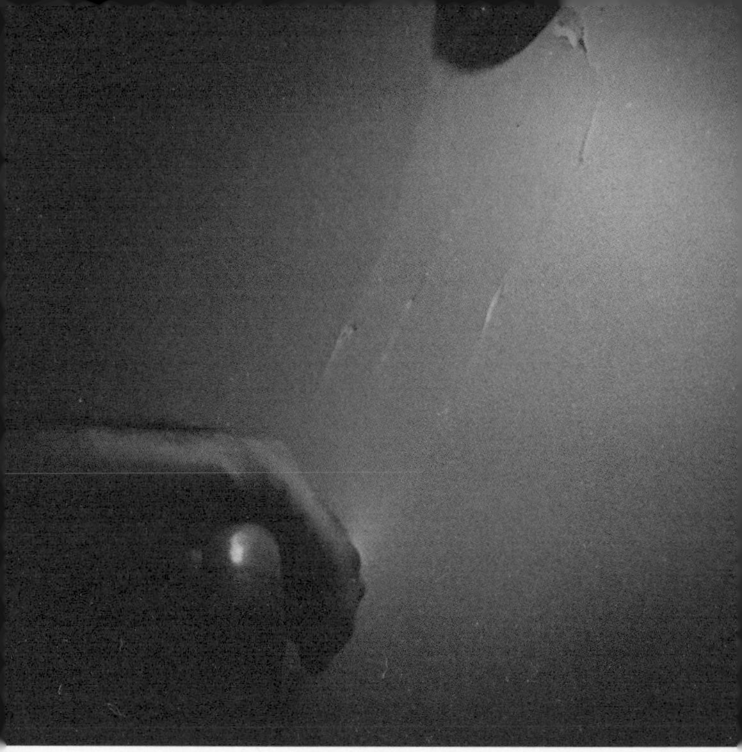

If agreed, negotiate the distance in this chase. Eventually, the prey stops, surrendering to the hunter. That stop might (or might not) be where things happen.

A possible conversation is valid, though not necessary. And that's that. Done.

03. Odyssey Theatre

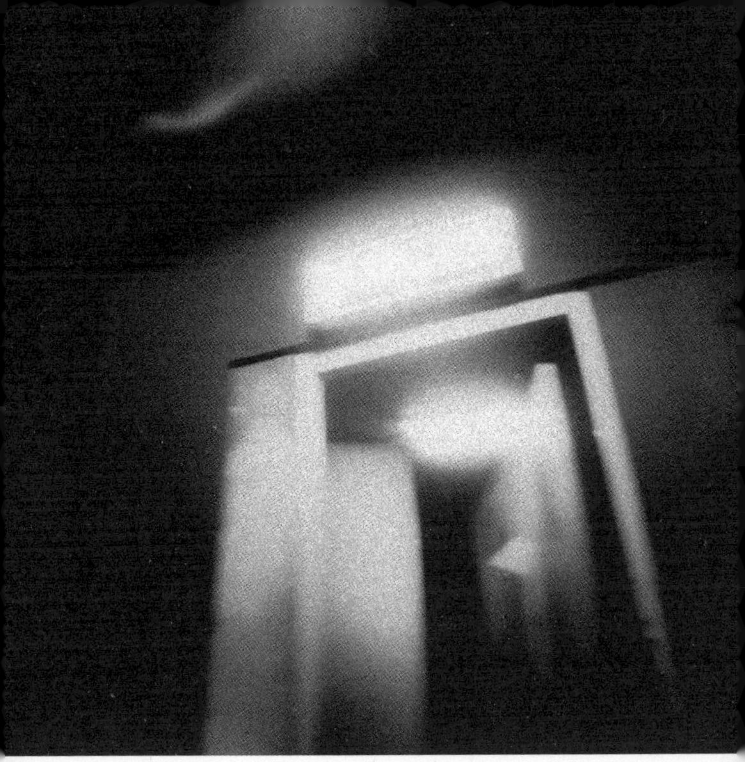

Cleanliness: 2/10
Safety: 4/10
Crowd: 6/10

It has only one screen.

Action spots: at the back of the room, up in the balcony, next to the ticket booth (ground floor), and the bathrooms (obviously).

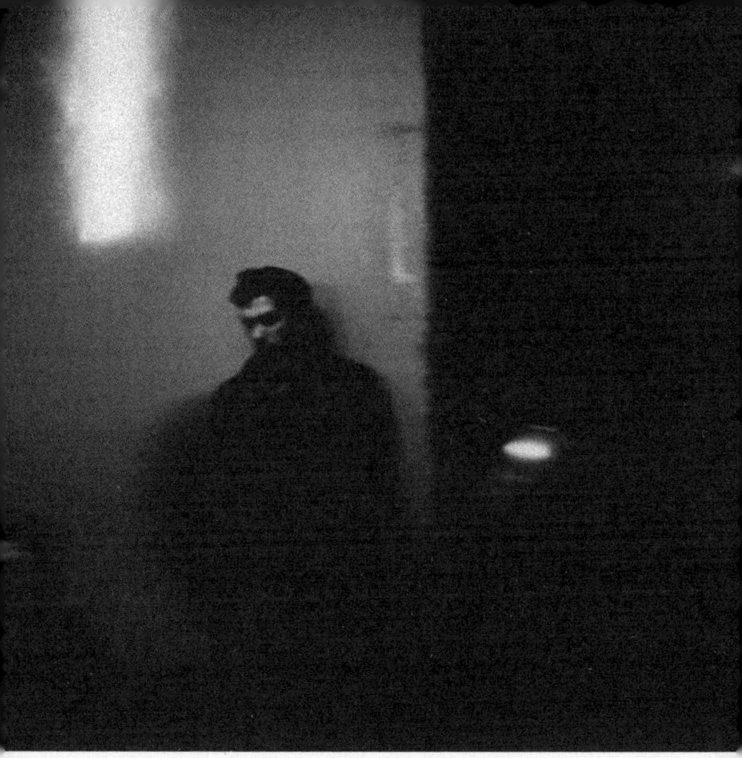

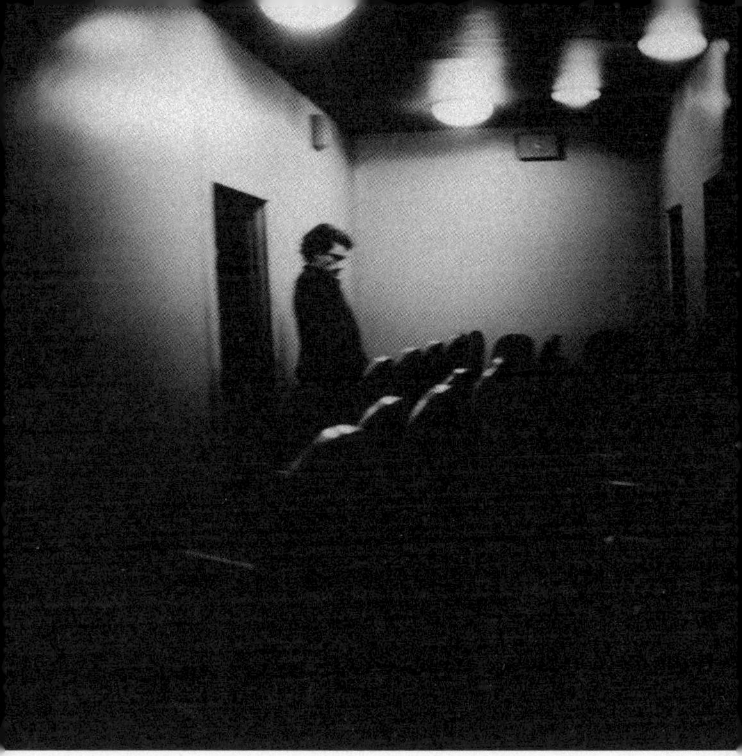

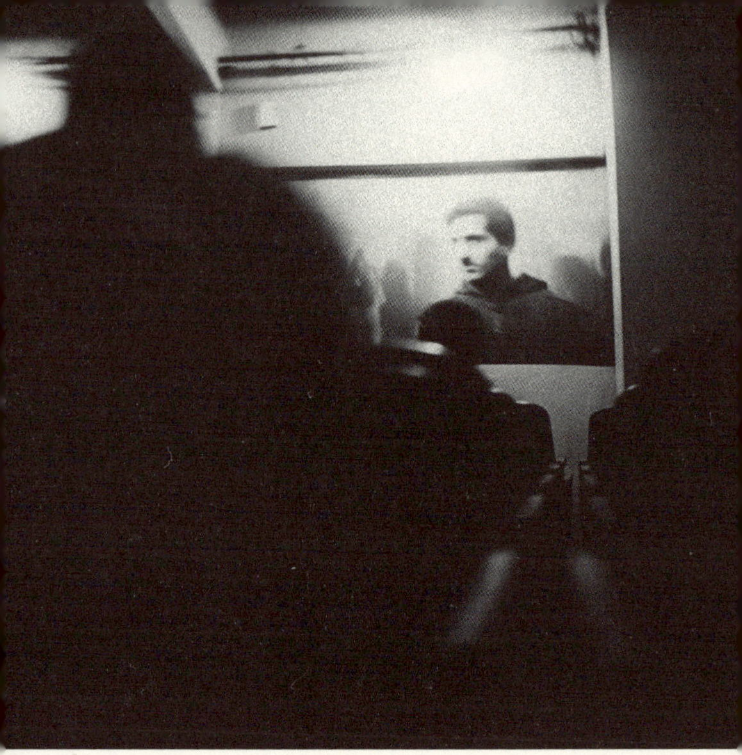

DL workers go there around 3 PM.
Plus, the old men who pay to touch or blow.

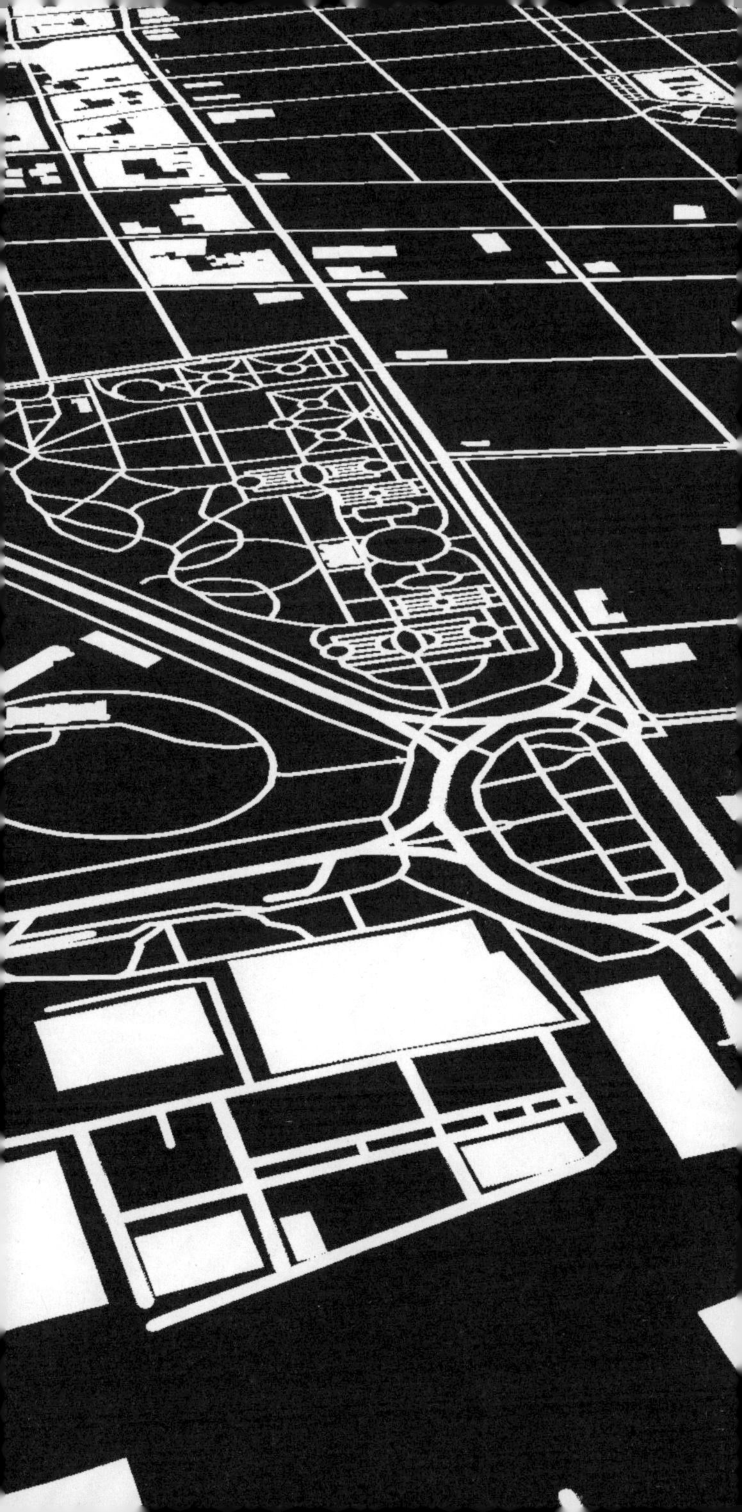

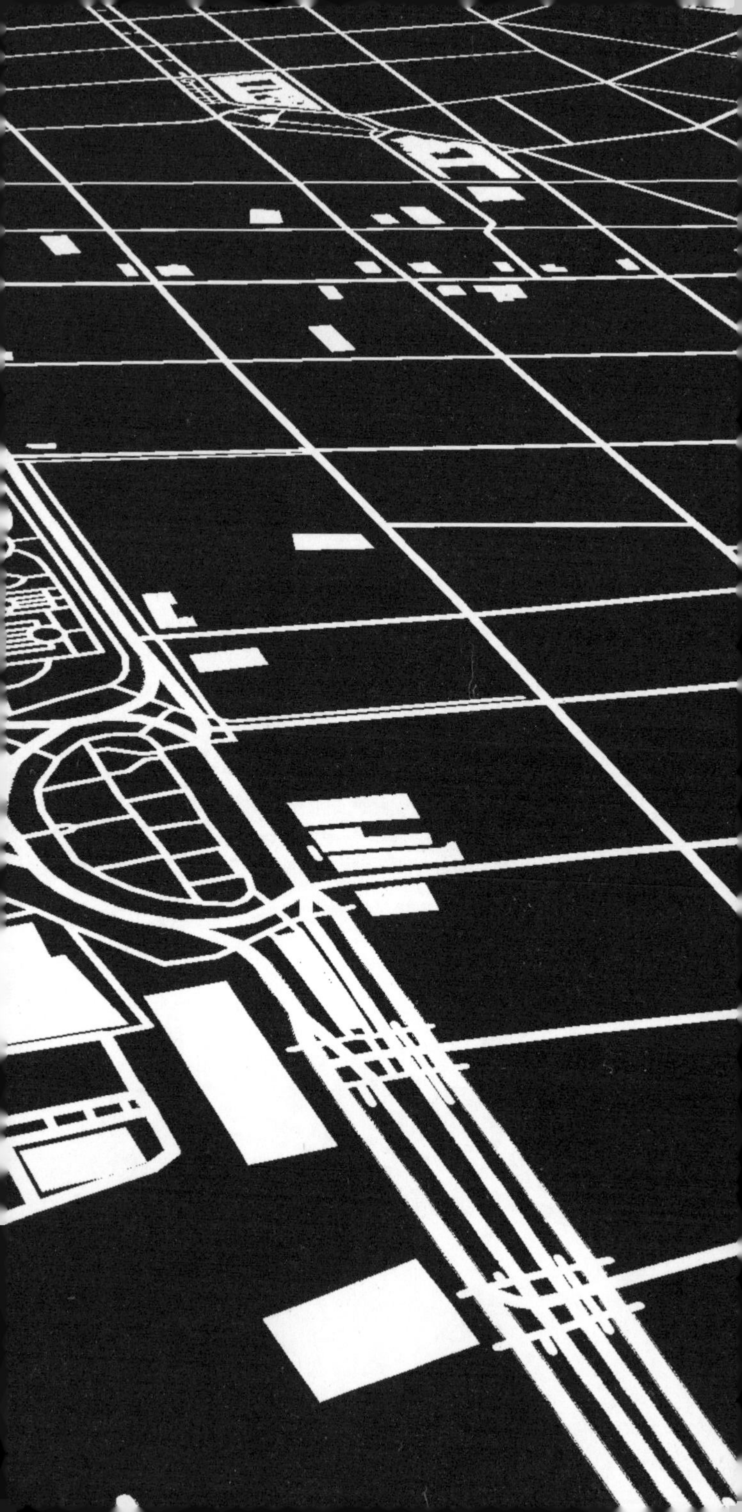

04. Mr. Garage Gym

05. Luxus Sex Shop

06. Hidalgo Subway Station

04. Mr. Garage Gym

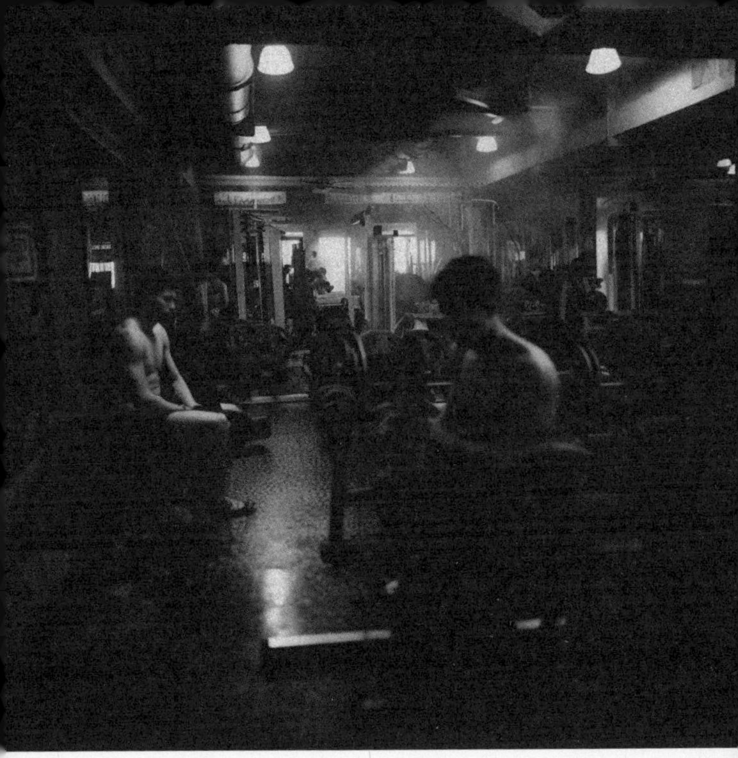

One of the few 24/7 gyms in the city. The machines need fixing, but overall, there's a good crowd and even better hookups.

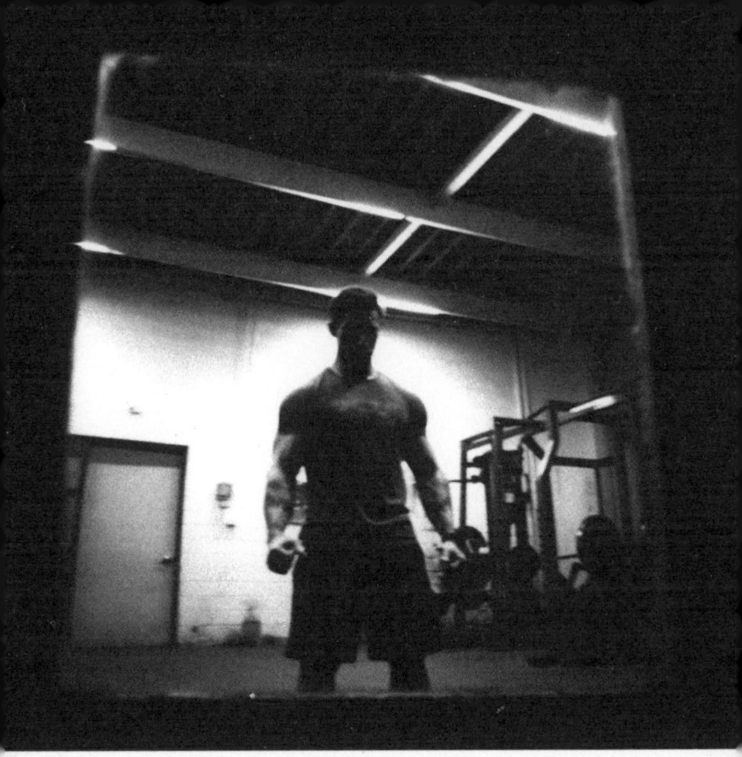

The cleaning staff knows the deal in the showers, but be discreet; there's always someone who has nothing to do with it.

Some curtains have holes to check if there's interest on the other side.

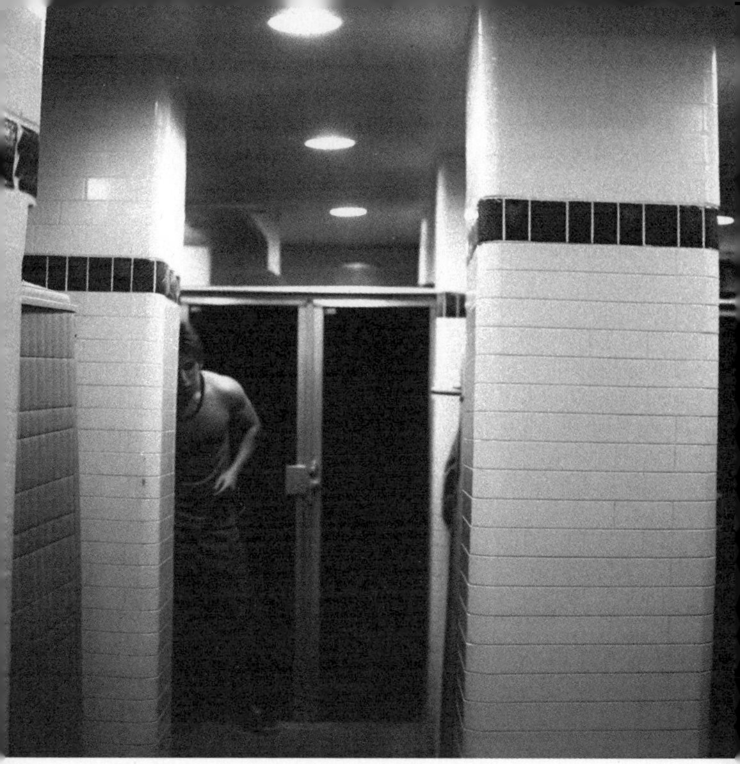

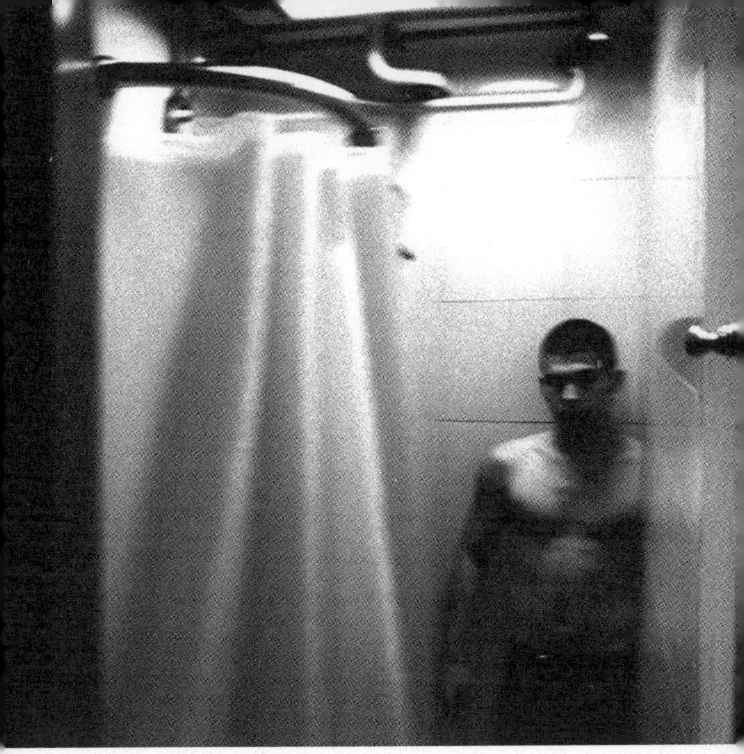

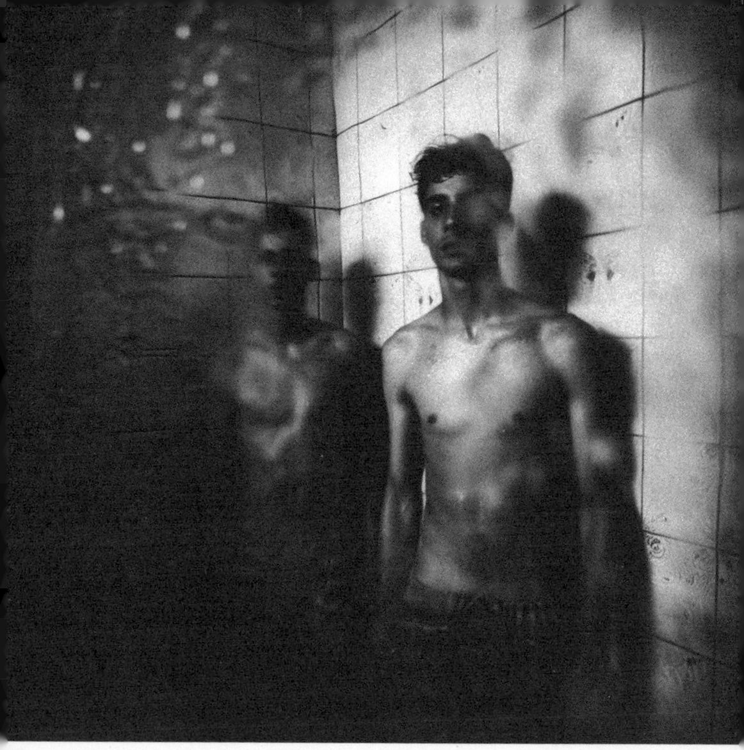

05. Luxus Sex Shop

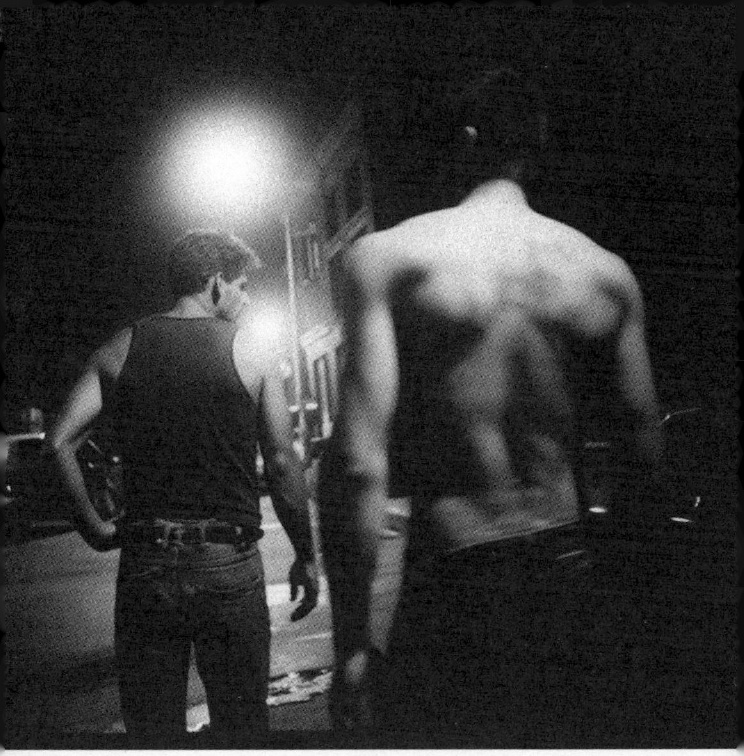

Back of Quorum Gallery, Store 59. Big place. Closes at 2 AM.

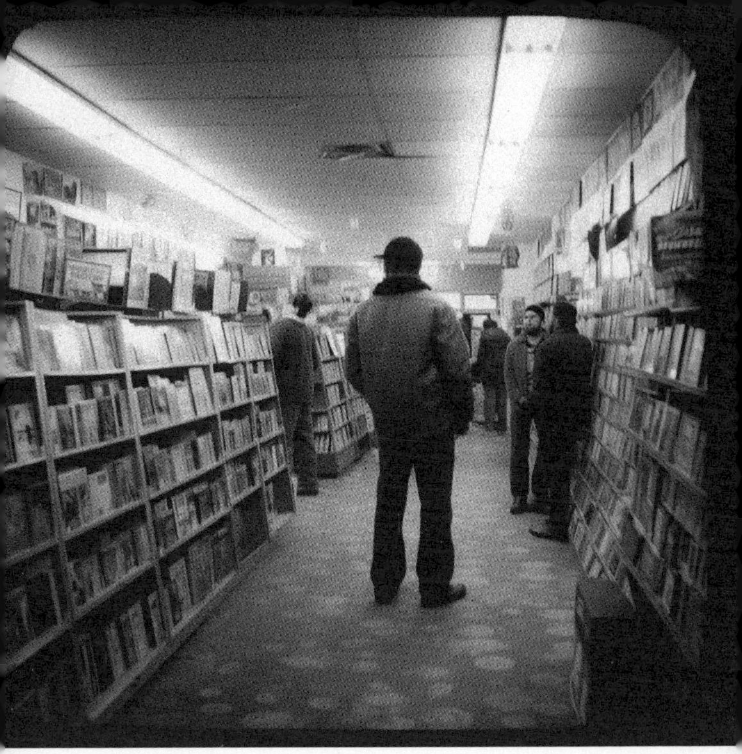

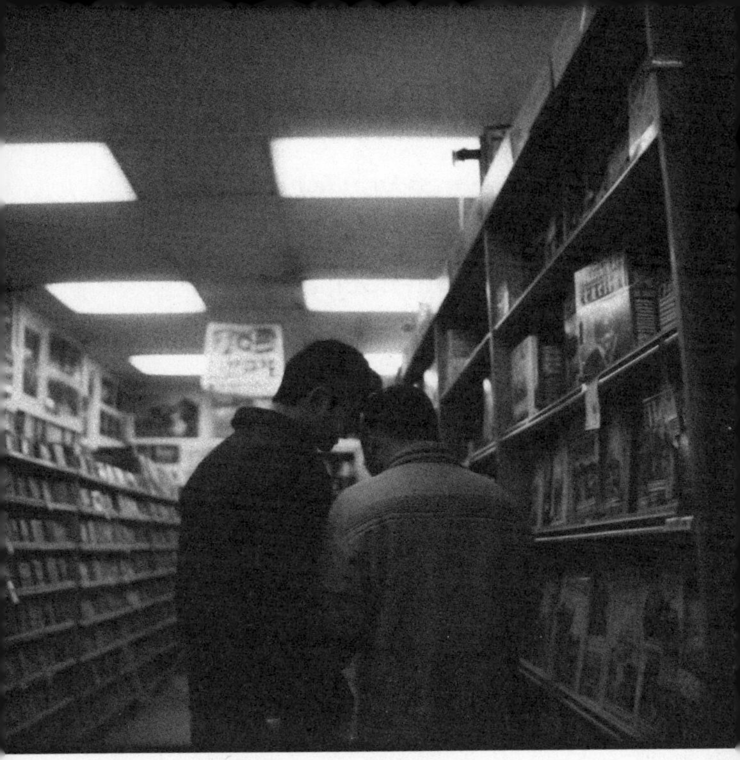

First grab a movie.
Take it up front.
Ask for a booth.

They'll only charge you for the booth time.

It's $150 for half an hour, $290 for an hour.

There are about 8 in total.

Hallway's usually cruising friendly too.

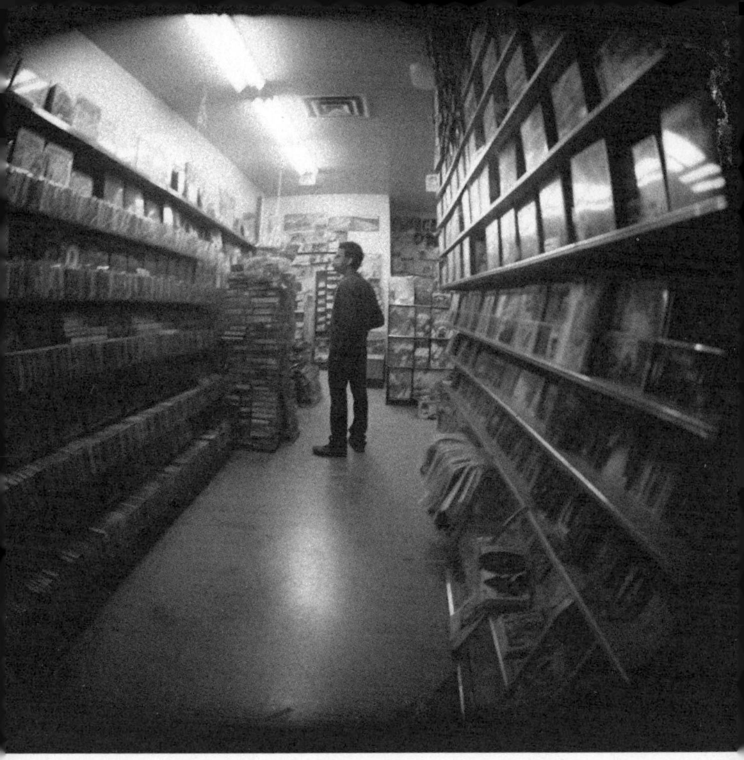

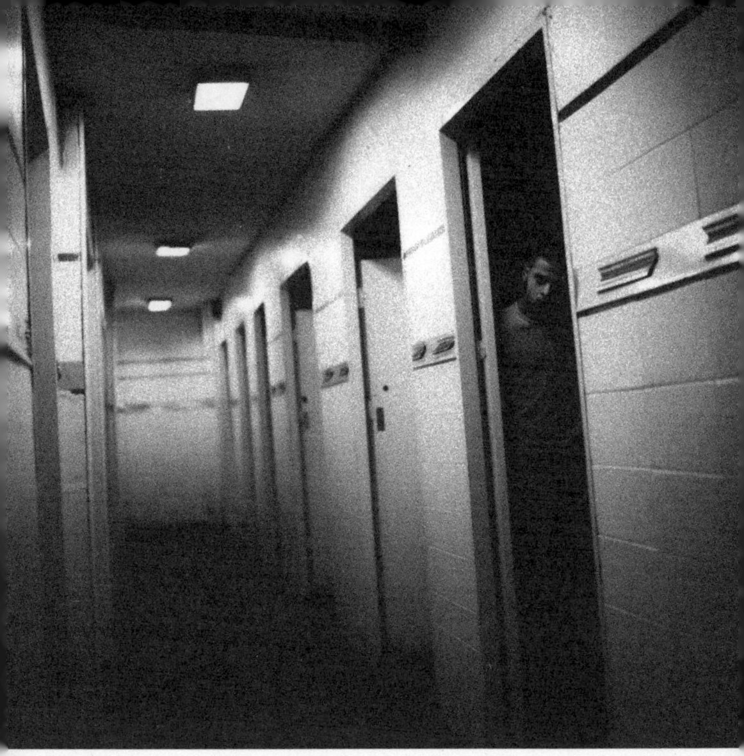

06. Hidalgo Subway Station

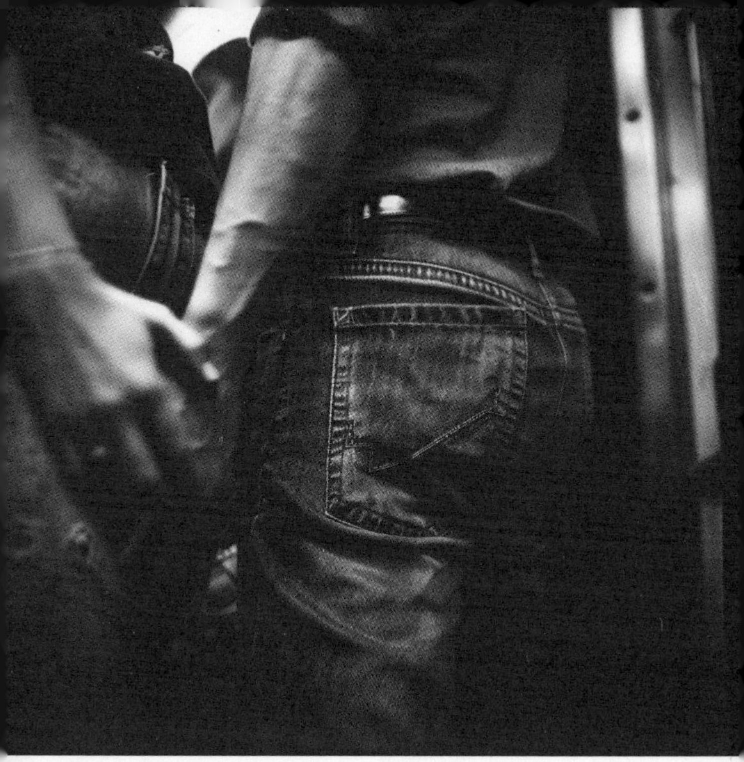

**It always goes down in the last car.
I don't know why — but it's always the last one. Even in other cities I've cruised.**

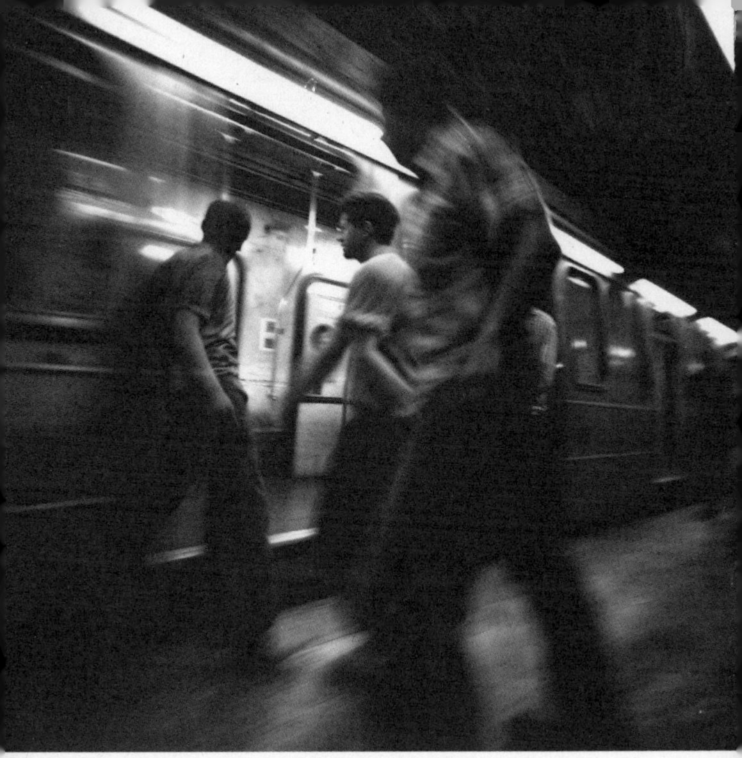

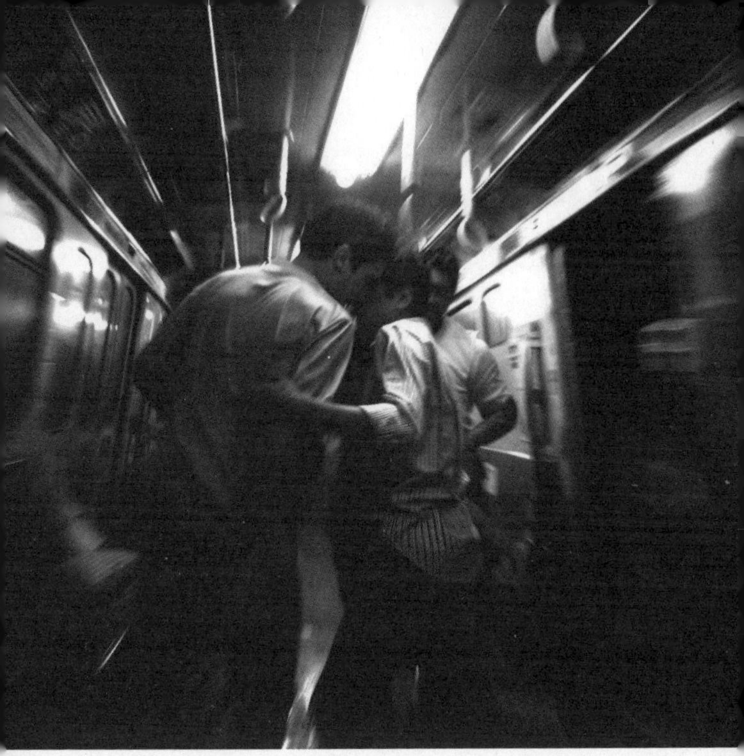

The Signals

- **The Empty Seat Gamble:** He sits next to you even when the car isn't full. Legs spread. Thigh against thigh. No pullback.

- **The Pole Grip:** Hands too close on the same metal bar. Fingers flex, grip tightens, releases slow.

- **The Window Reflection Game:** No direct staring, just quick glances in the glass. Watching without watching.

- **The Knee Bounce:** Seated, foot tapping, knee bouncing, restless. A signal.

- **The Clothes Adjust:** A slow pull at the waistband. A thumb grazing a belt loop. A stretch that lifts the shirt just enough.

There are two windows: rush hour and the last trains before shutdown.

Rush hour is perfect for friction. For feeling someone's bulge press against yours. For a quick grope. A hand sliding under a t-shirt. Maybe a grab of ass. But that's about it. No full moves. This city's rush hour gets brutal — bodies packed so tight it's easier to hide in the noise of it all. Nobody can really tell who's touching who. And half the time, nobody cares.

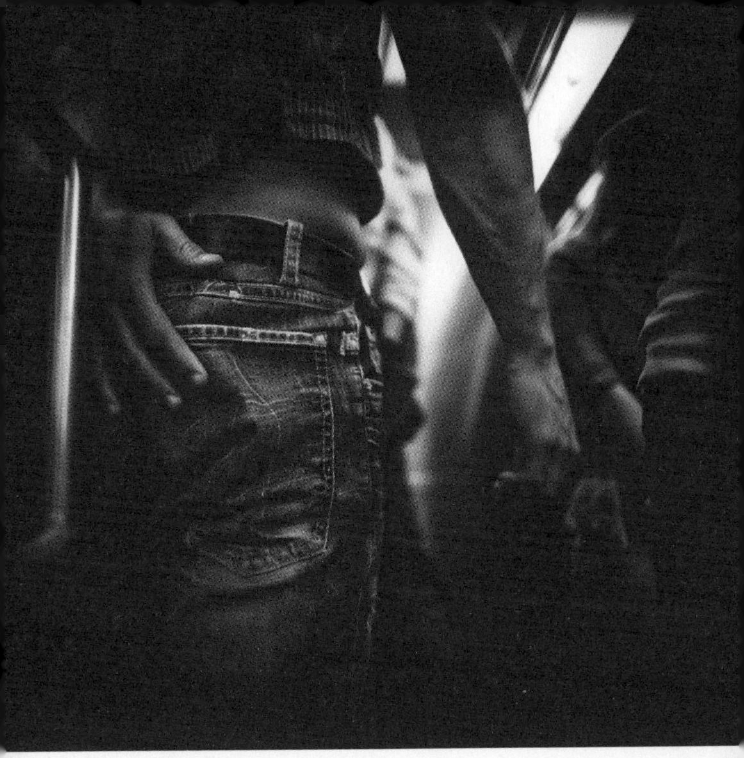

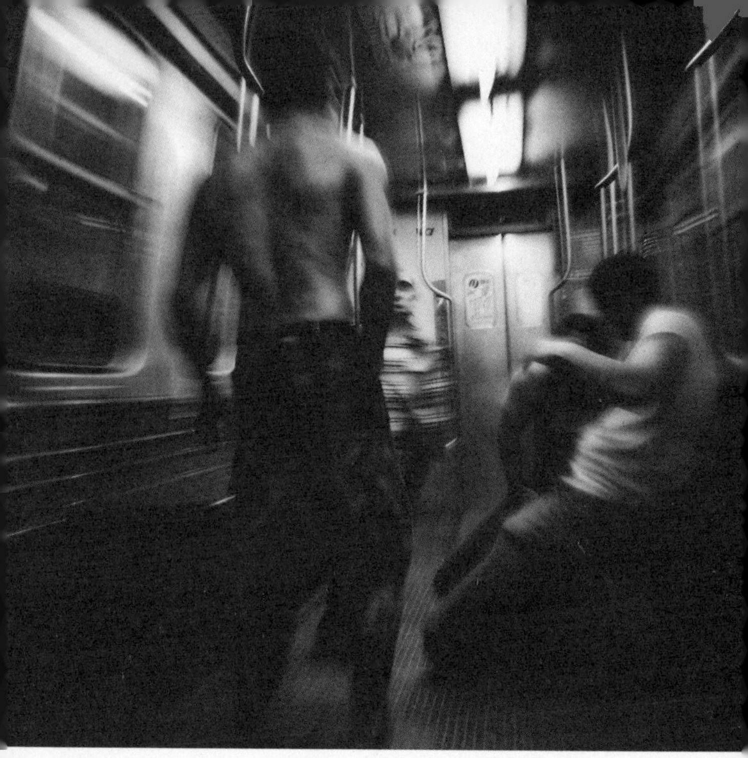

Late-night trains are different. Dark.

You step into the last car and everyone pretends they're just riding home. For like two seconds. They clock you. You clock them. If you stay, if you don't pull out your phone, it starts.

Hands. Cocks out. Mouths moving. I've seen guys get fucked between two stops.

It's fast. Brutal. You get a minute, maybe two, before the next station lights up the car again. You either get off quick or you wait for the next window.

That's how it goes.

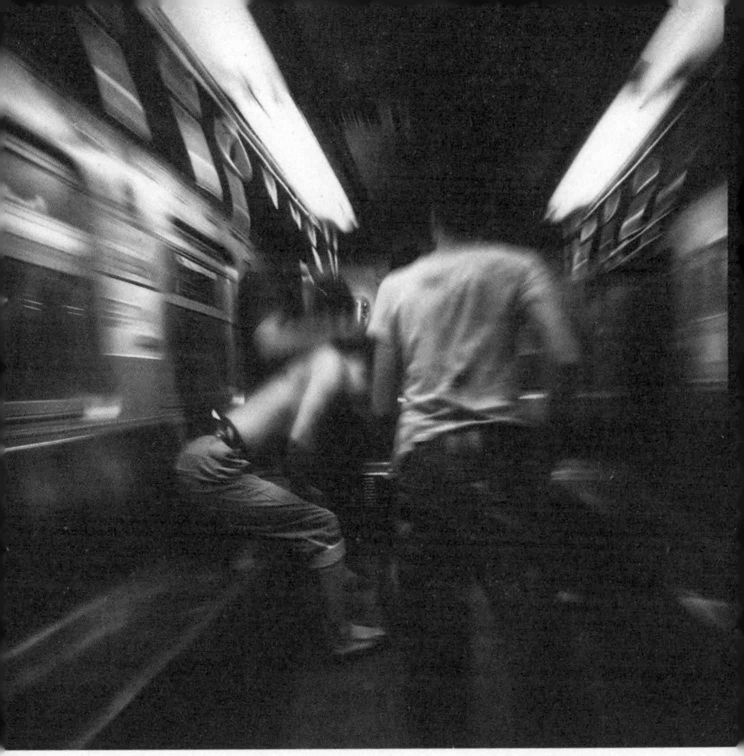

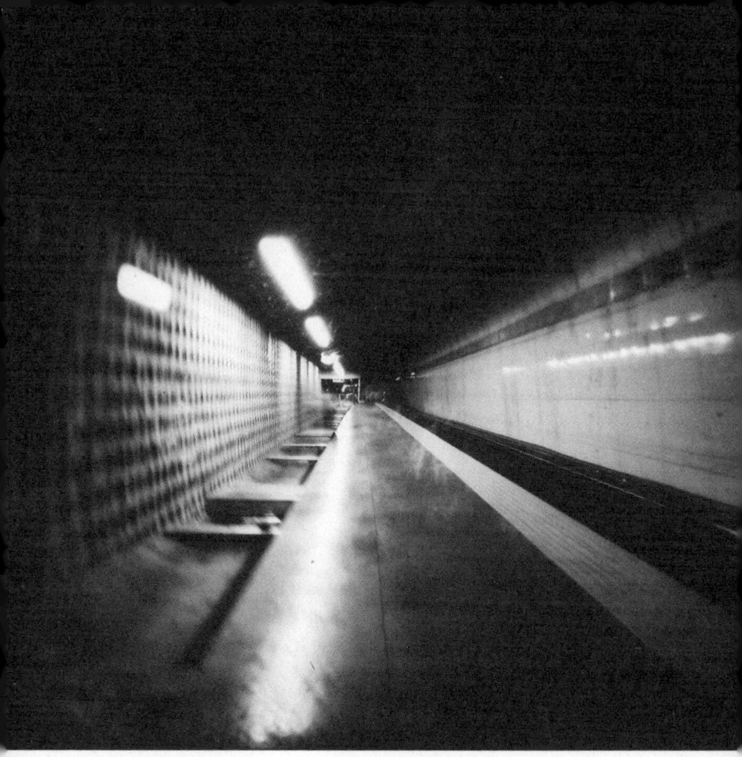

Intermission: Leftovers

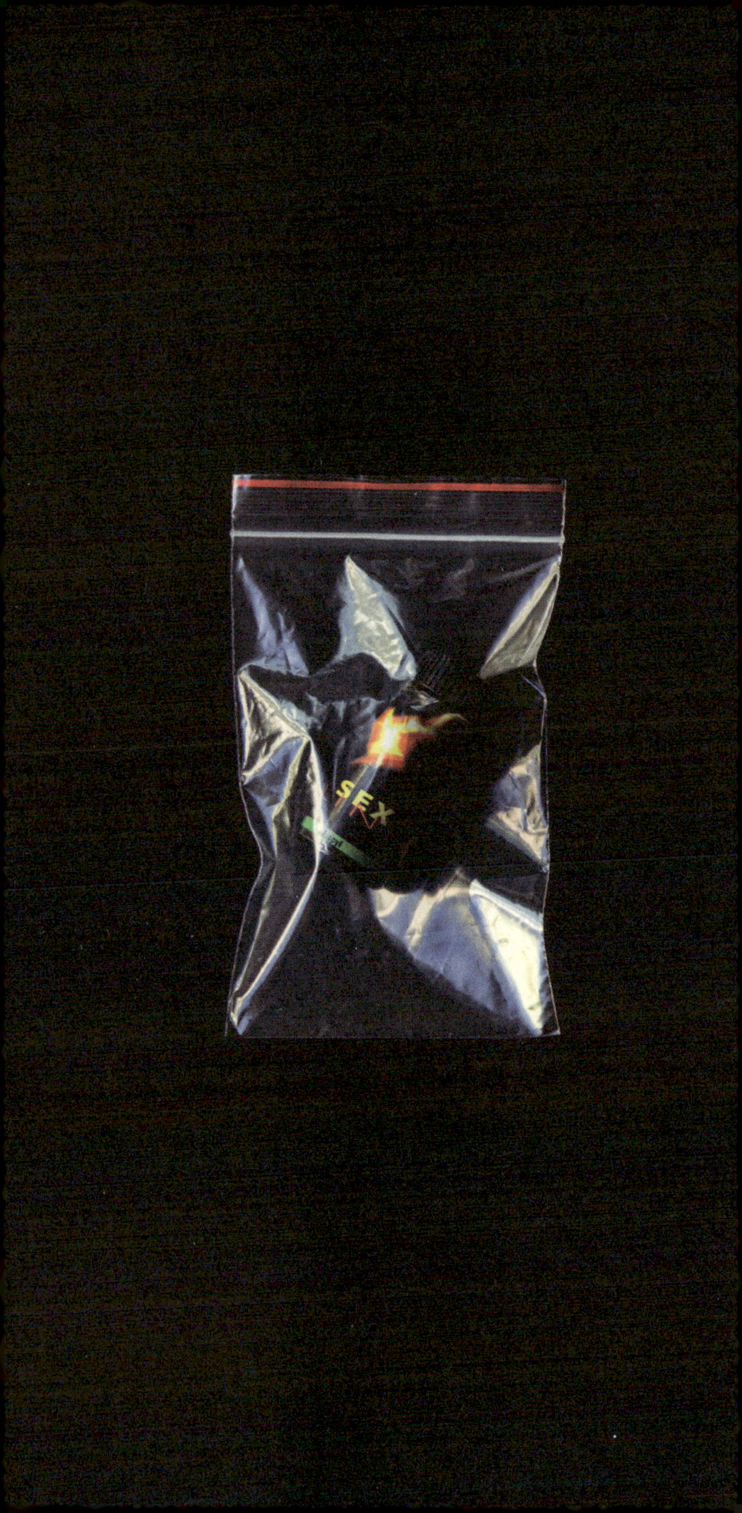
SEX

ID	#1
LOCATION	LOVE BEACH CAVE
MEASUREMENTS	6x2 cm
NOTES	EMPTY 'SEX' BRAND POPPERS BOTTLE.
DATE	01.03.2024

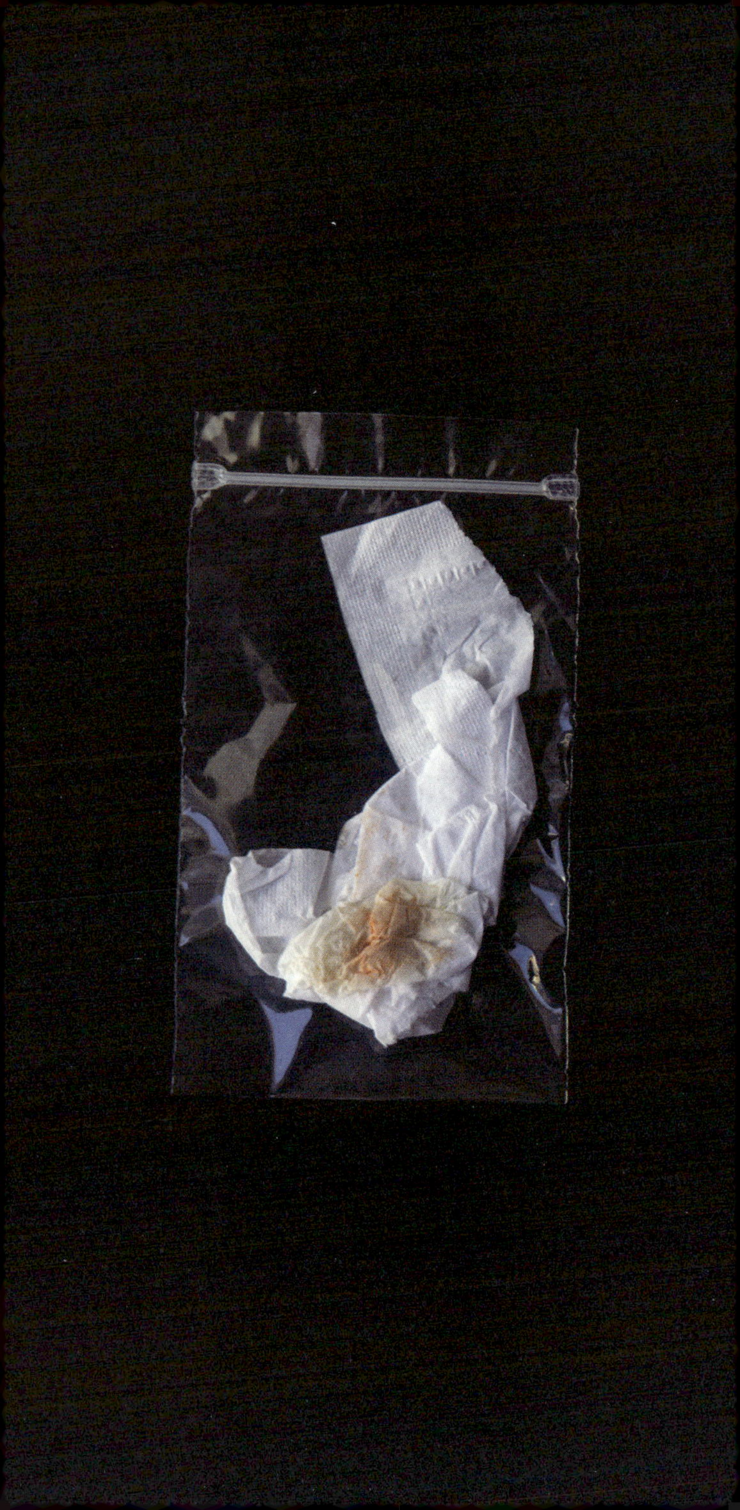

ID	#2
LOCATION	SANTA ANA PARK
MEASUREMENTS	7x8 cm (IRREGULAR)
NOTES	CRUMPLED PAPER NAPKIN FOUND ON THE FLOOR. REMAINS OF WET SHIT AND POSSIBLE BLOOD.
DATE	01.15.2024

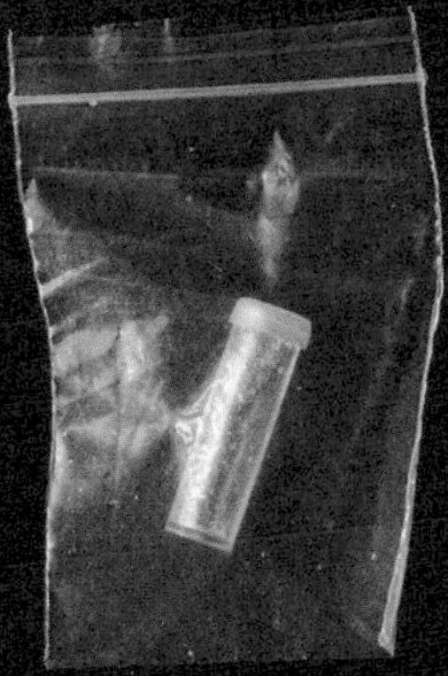

ID	#3
LOCATION	HONDA CIVIC - LEZAMA PARK
MEASUREMENTS	1x3.5 cm
NOTES	CLOSED TRANSPARENT PLASTIC BOTTLE. OPAQUE MDMA RESIDUE INSIDE. GIFT FROM A GUY AFTER BLOWING HIM.
DATE	02.08.2024

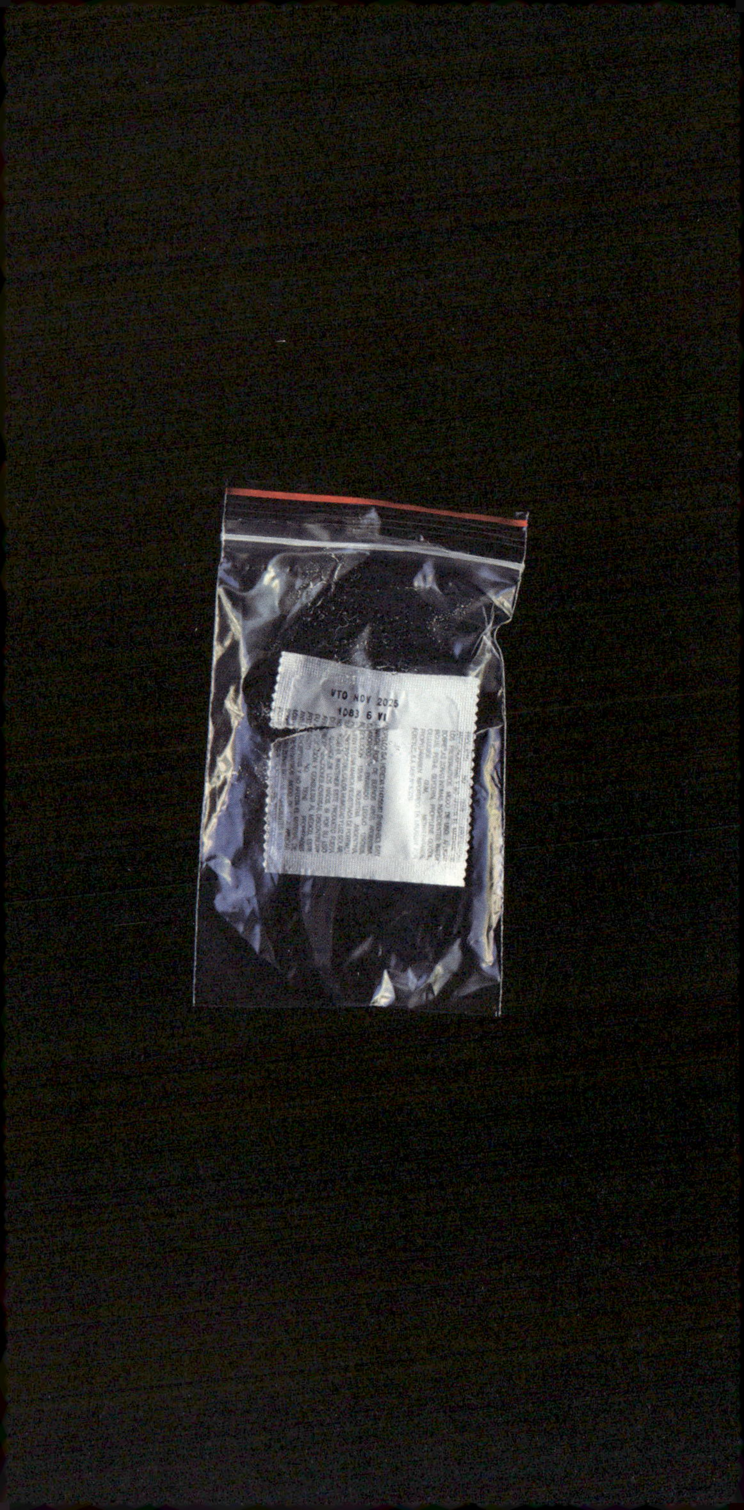
VTO NOV 2025
1083 6 VI

ID	#4
LOCATION	LUXUS SEX SHOP
MEASUREMENTS	4.5x4.5 cm
NOTES	OPEN CONDOM WRAPPER WITH EXPIRATION DATE NOV. 2026. GENERIC BRAND PROVIDED BY THE MINISTRY OF HEALTH.
DATE	03.19.2024

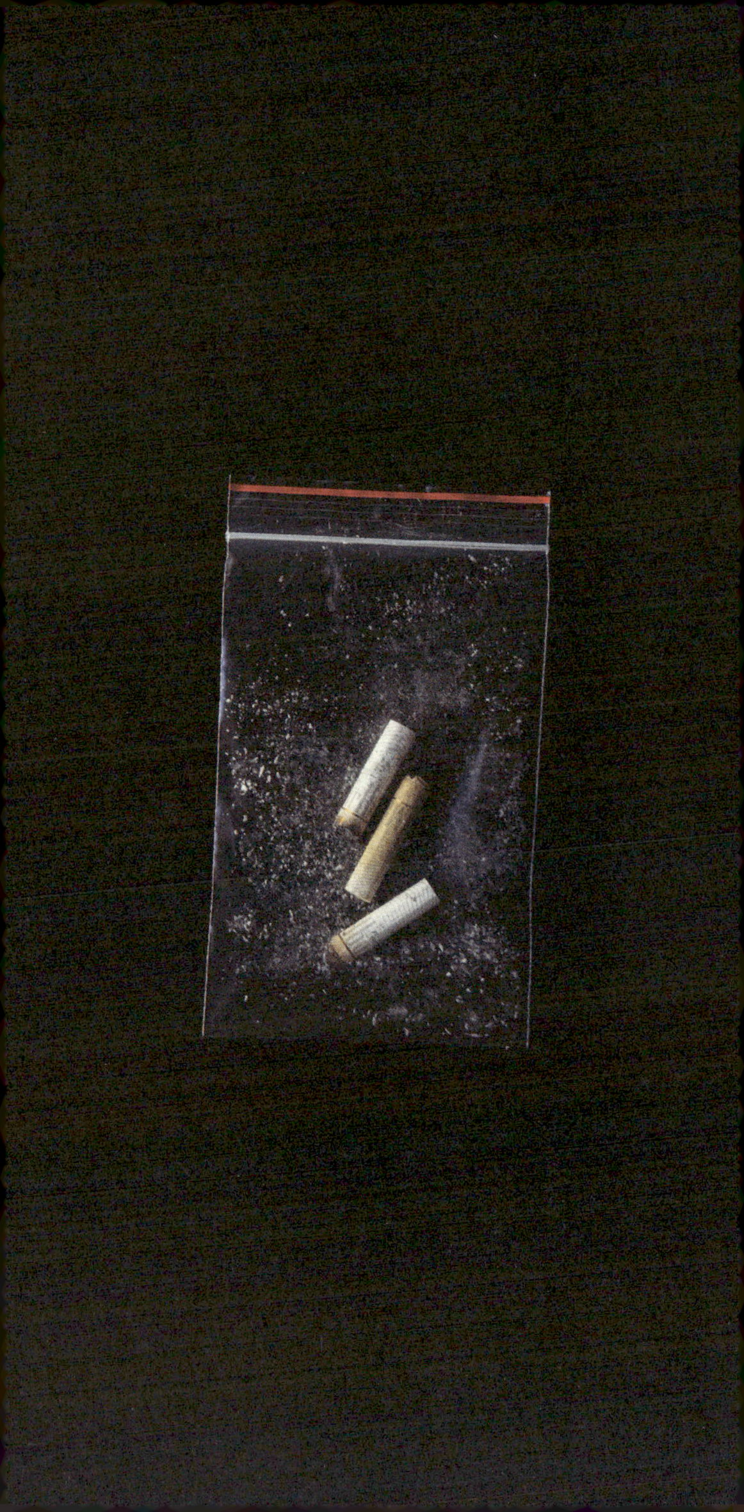

ID	#5
LOCATION	ODYSSEY THEATRE
MEASUREMENTS	3x1 cm APROX EACH
NOTES	3 MARLBORO GOLD CIGA-RETTE BUTTS FOUND UNDER THE SAME CINEMA SEAT.
DATE	04.08.2024

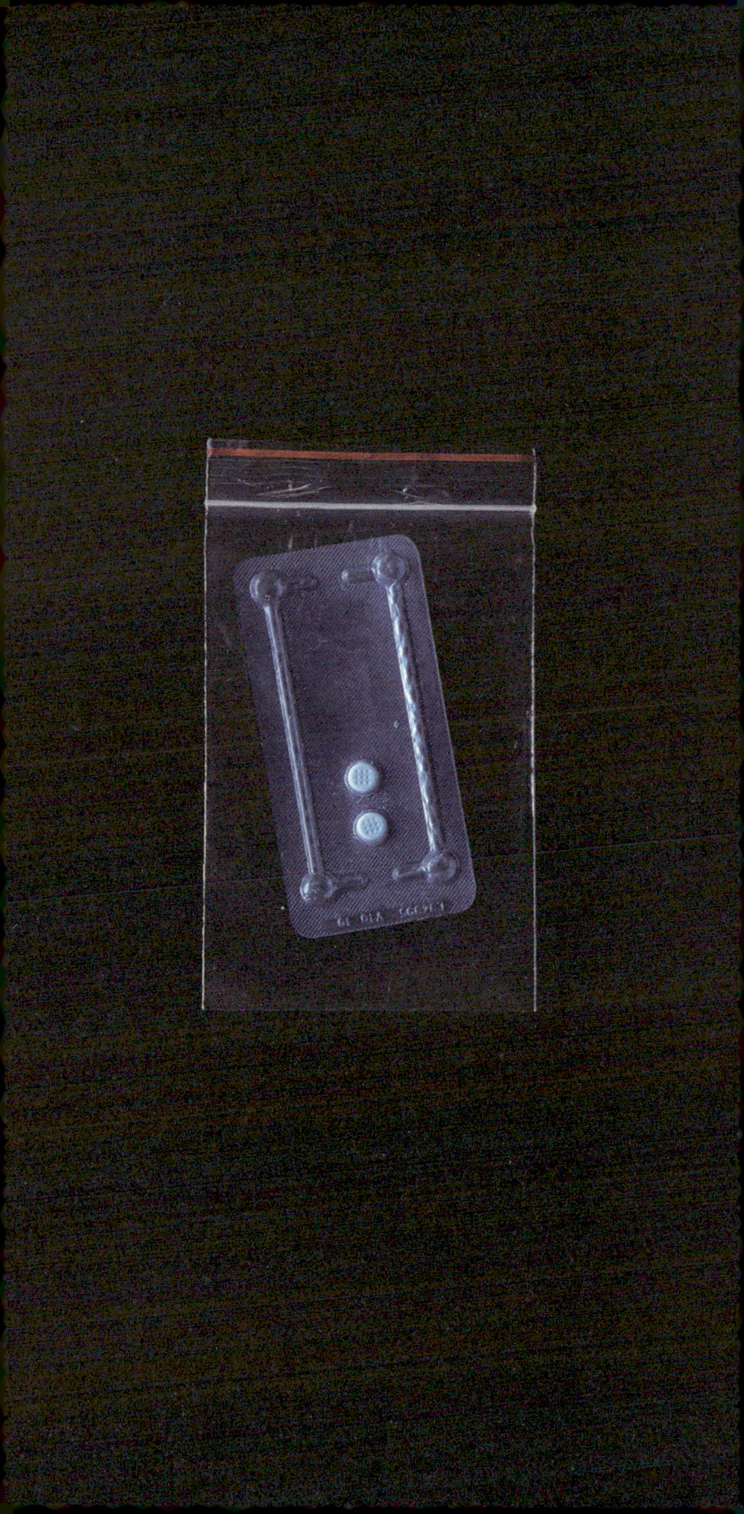

ID	#6
LOCATION	LAVALLE VIP CYBER
MEASUREMENTS	4x8 cm
NOTES	BLISTER PACK WITH ‘MEDICAL SAMPLE’ LEGEND ON THE BACK. CONTAINS TWO 100mg SILDENAFIL PILLS EXPIRED IN 2019.
DATE	04.29.2024

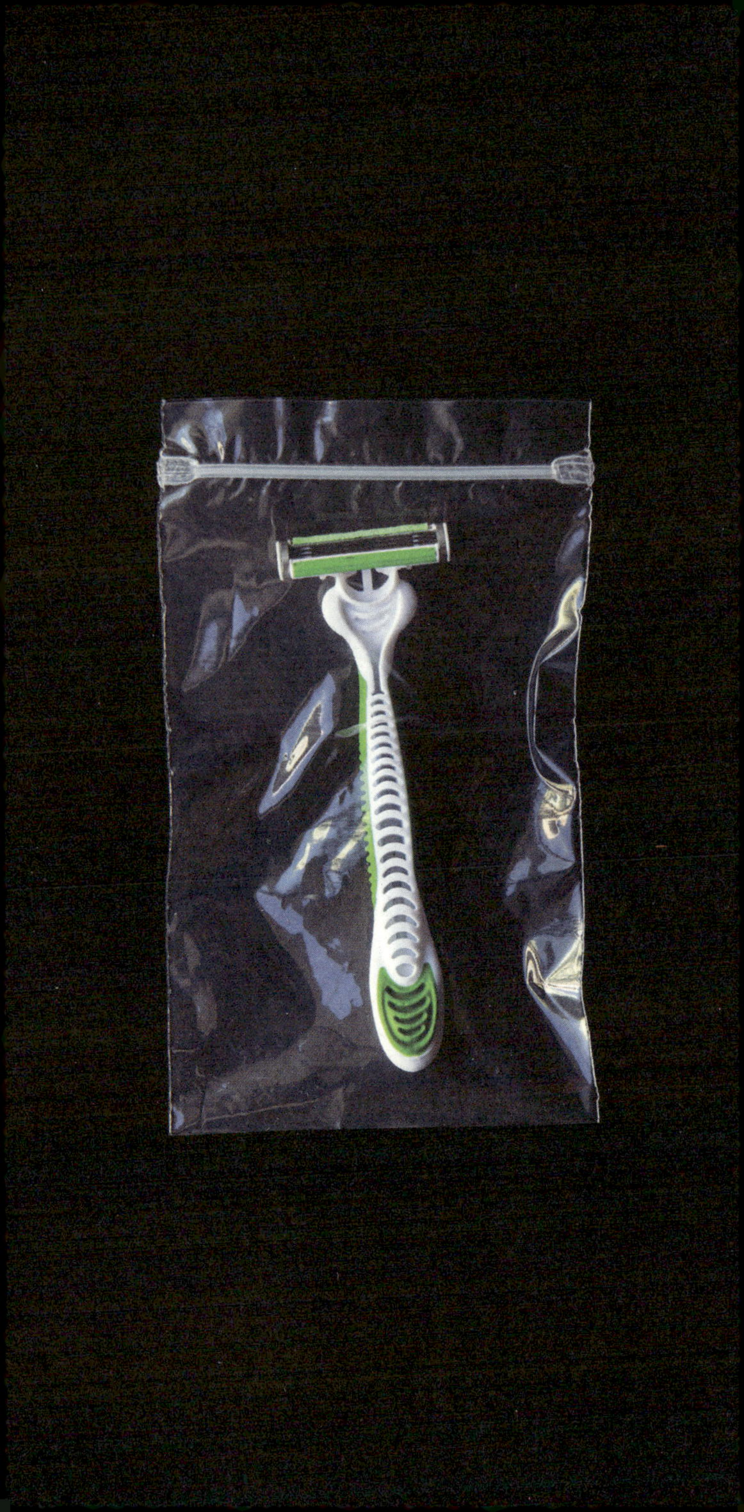

ID	#7
LOCATION	MR. GARAGE GYM
MEASUREMENTS	4x10cm
NOTES	USED, UNBRANDED RAZOR FOUND IN THE GYM SHOWERS.
DATE	05.05.2024

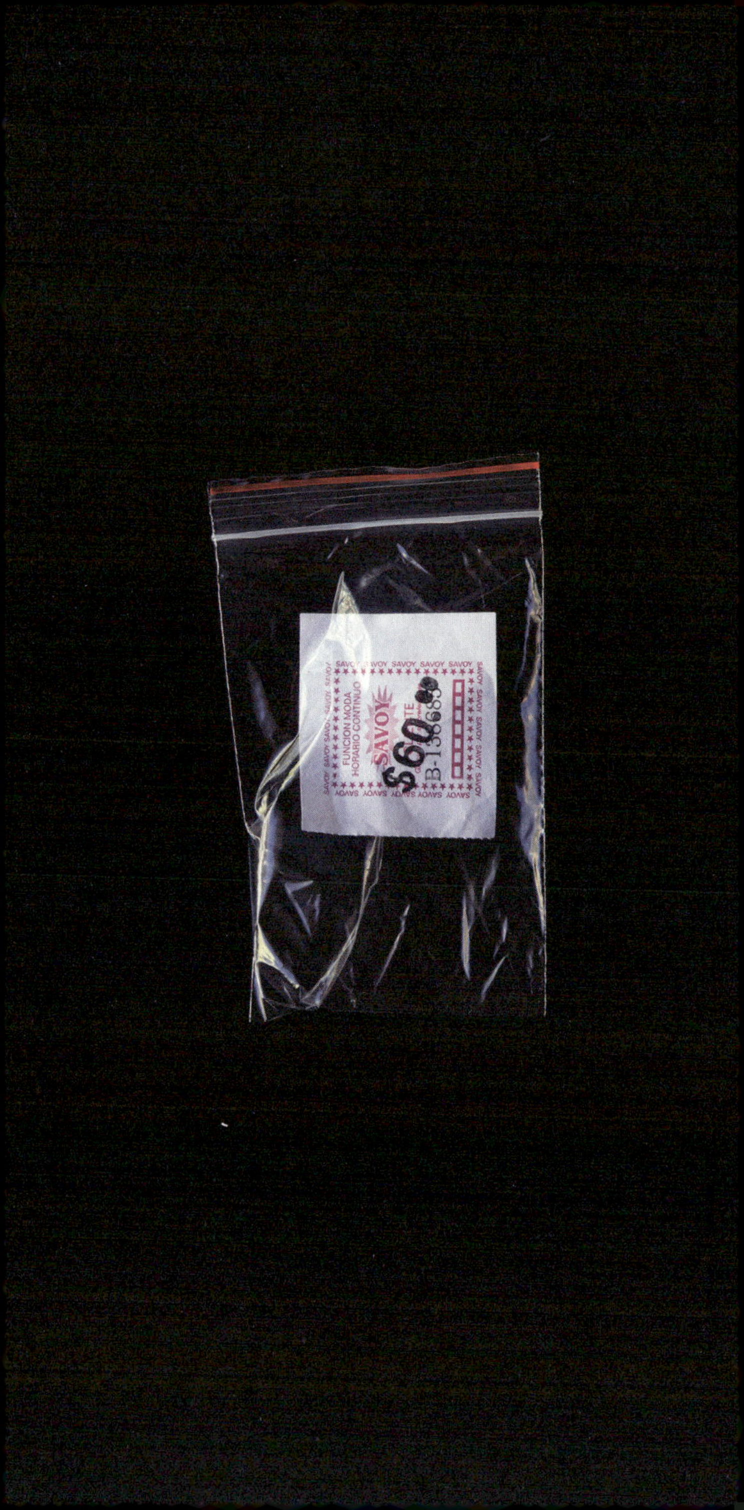
SAVOY
FUNCION MODA
HORARIO CONTINUO
$60

ID	#8
LOCATION	CINE SAVOY
MEASUREMENTS	4x8 cm
NOTES	CINE SAVOY TICKET WITH THE INSCRIPTION 'CONTINUOUS SHOW' AND ITS PRICE OF $60 STAMPED IN INK.
DATE	05.15.2024

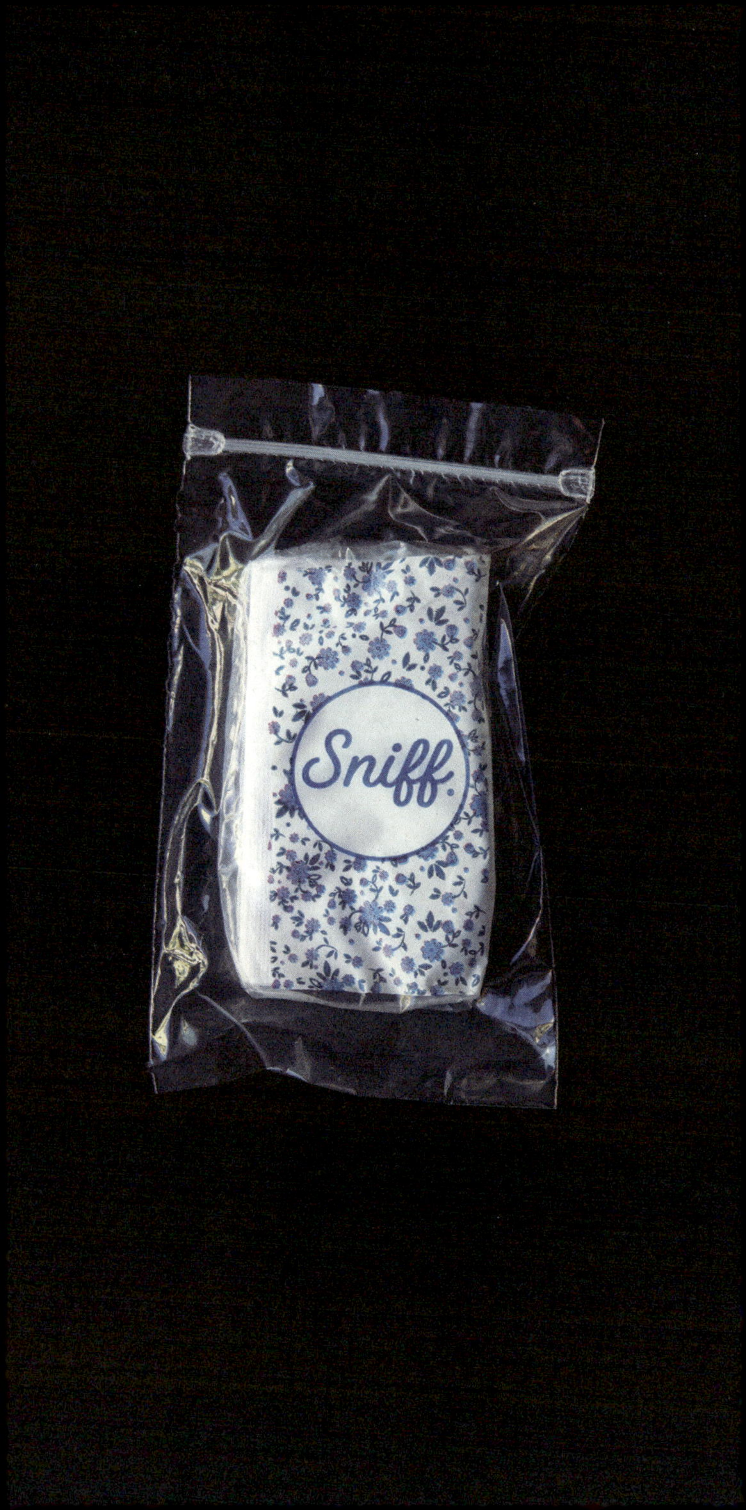
Sniff.

ID	#9
LOCATION	WALMART PARKING LOT
MEASUREMENTS	5x10 cm
NOTES	OPEN PACK OF ‘SNIFF’ BRAND DISPOSABLE TISSUES.
DATE	06.10.2024

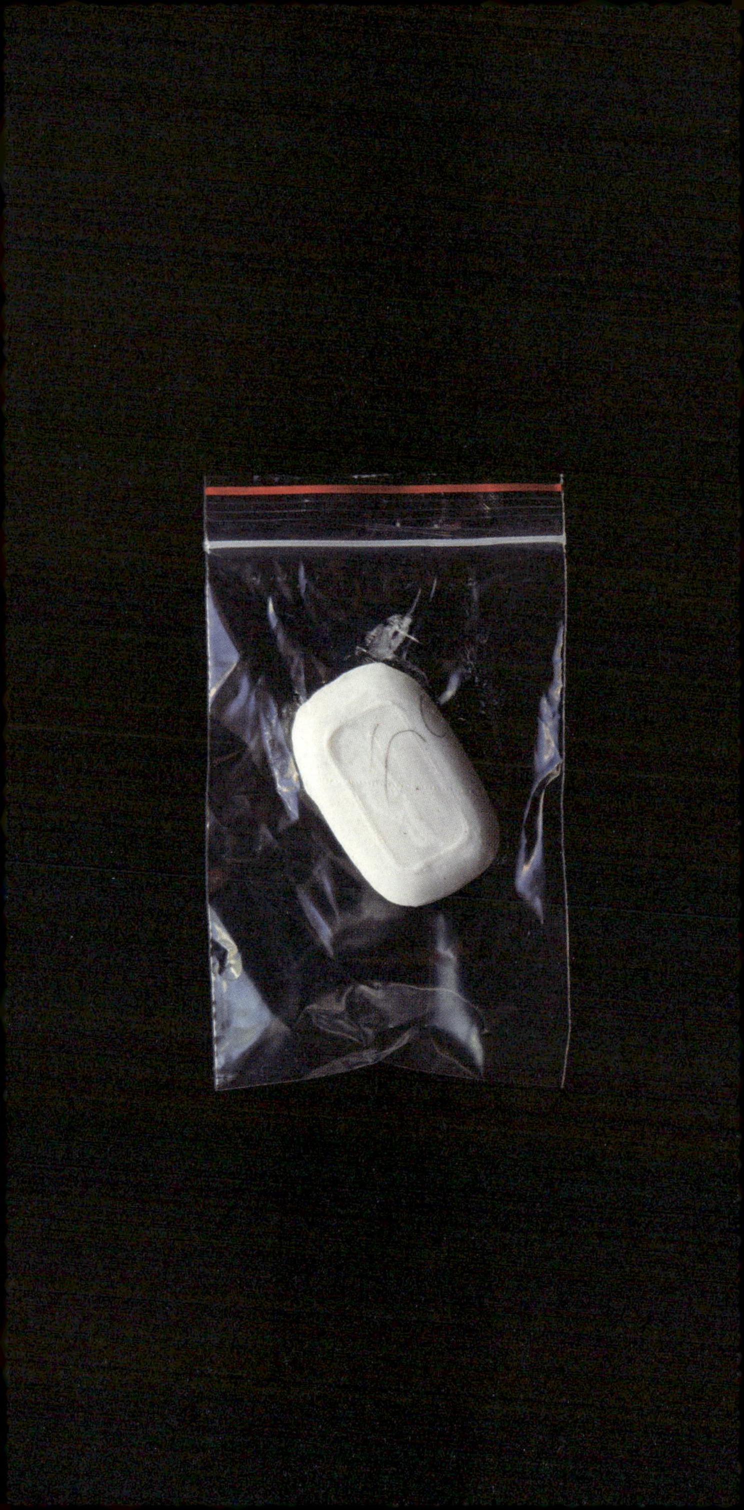

ID	#10
LOCATION	BAREFOOT HOTEL
MEASUREMENTS	3.5x5 cm
NOTES	WHITE SHOWER SOAP FROM THE HOTEL. SLIGHTLY USED AND DAMP. STILL HAS SOME HAIRS (POSSIBLY SCALP HAIRS) STUCK TO IT.
DATE	07.01.2024

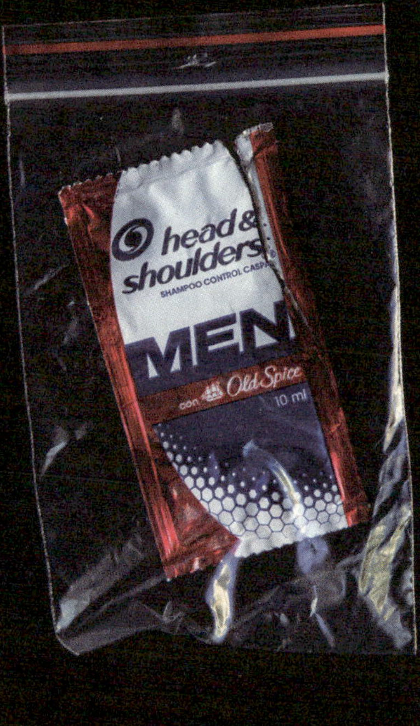
head &
shoulders
SHAMPOO CONTROL CASPA
MEN
con Old Spice
10 ml

ID	#11
LOCATION	GYM MR. GARAGE
MEASUREMENTS	4x8 cm
NOTES	OPEN HEAD & SHOULDERS 'MEN' SHAMPOO PACKET WITH LITTLE REMAINING CONTENT.
DATE	07.24.2024

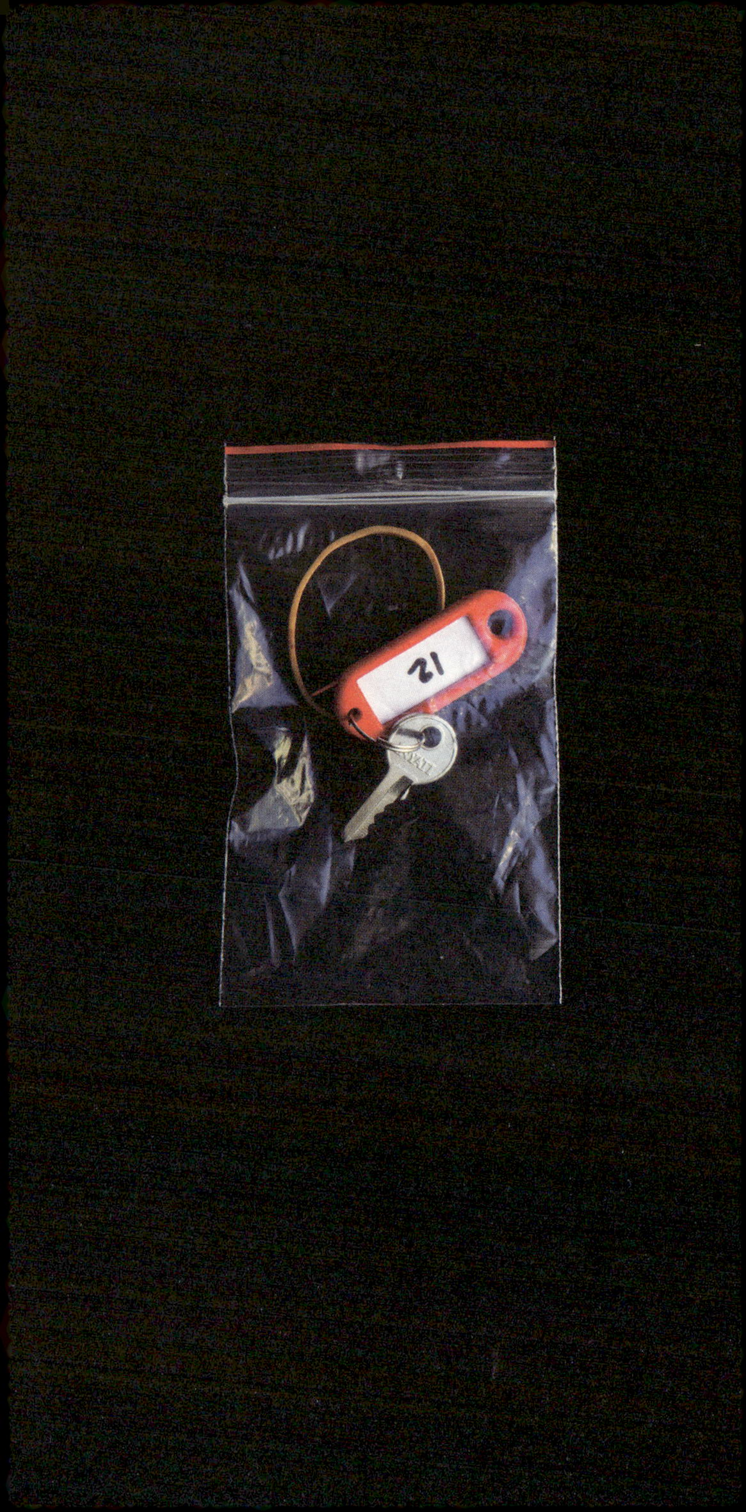

ID	#12
LOCATION	MADISON SPA
MEASUREMENTS	IRREGULAR
NOTES	LOCKER KEY WITH ITS TAG. NUMBER 12 HANDWRITTEN ON IT. GENERIC ELASTIC BAND ATTACHED TO THE KEYCHAIN.
DATE	08.01.2024

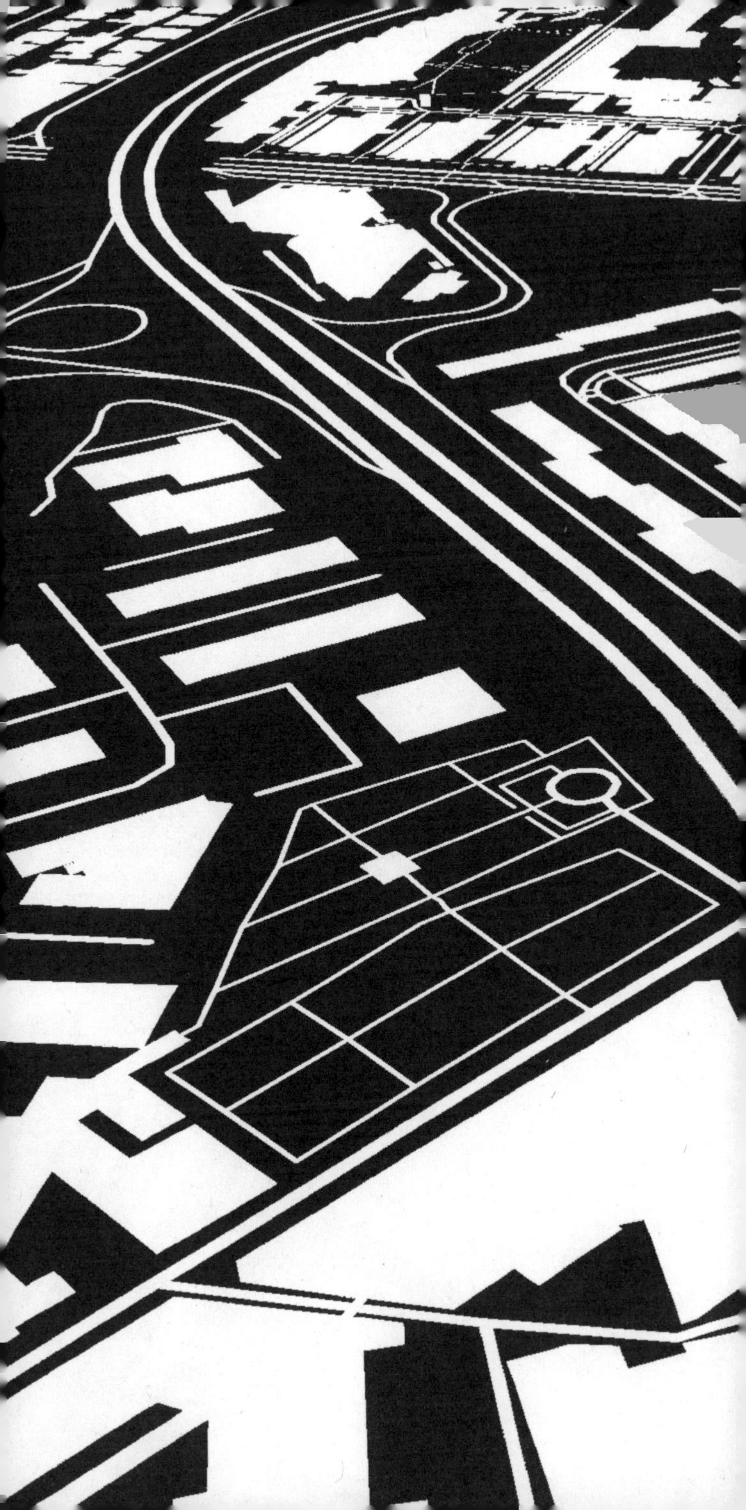

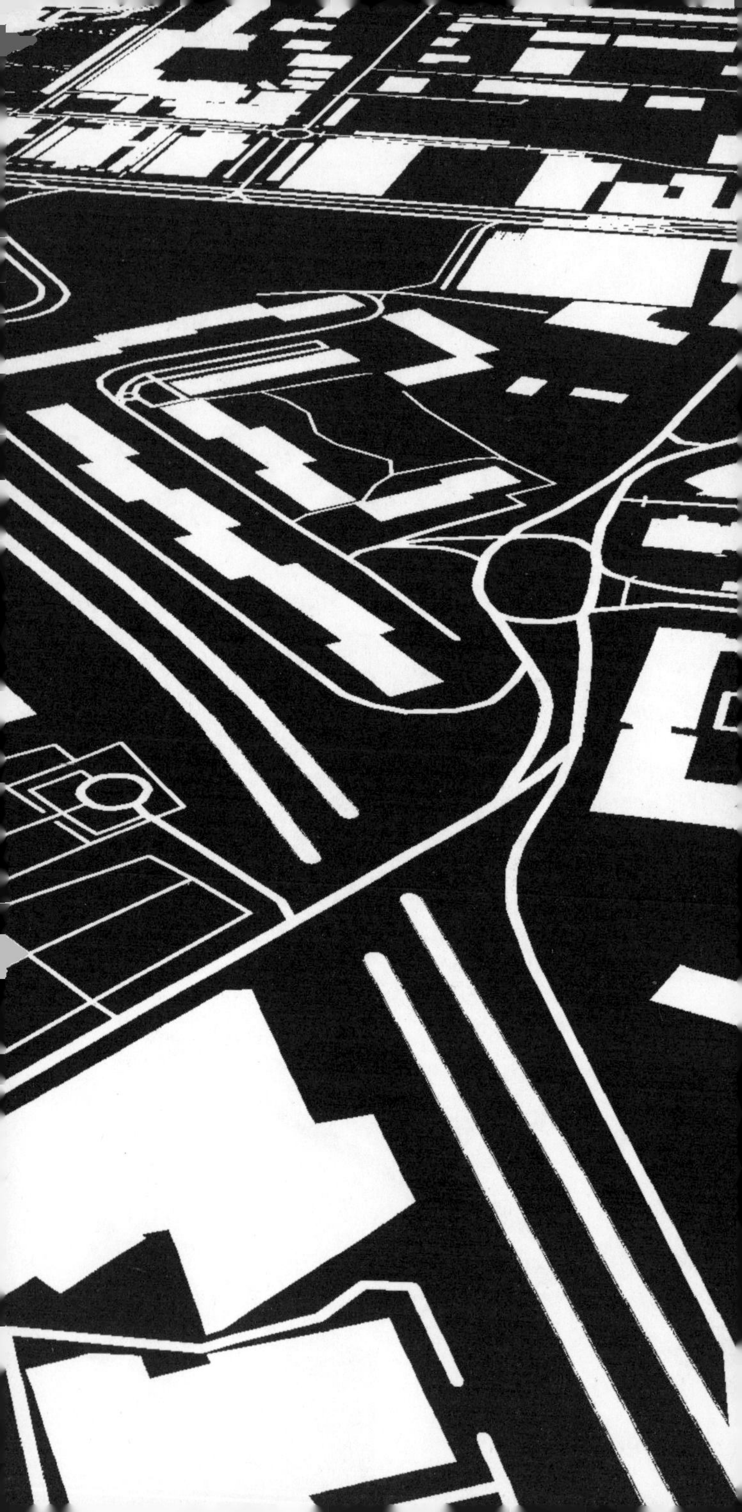

07. Santa Ana Forest

08. Lavalle VIP Cyber

07. Santa Ana Park

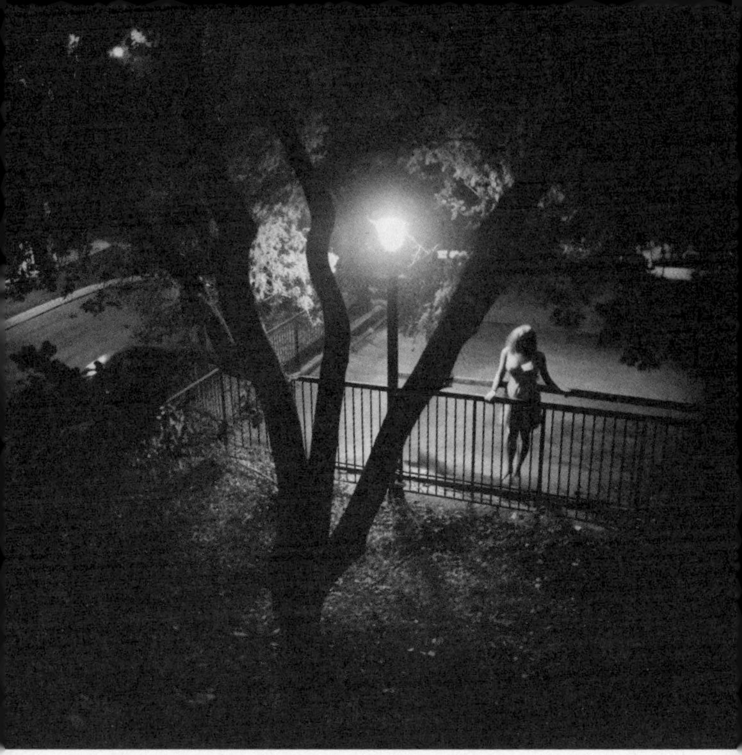

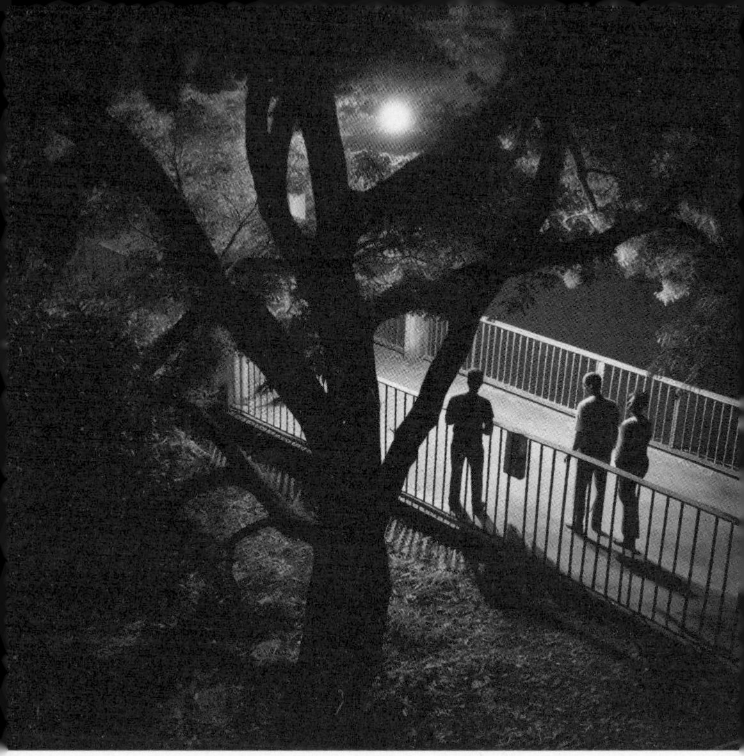

In recent years, the red-light district has gotten a bit more dangerous, but is still the best spot in the city.

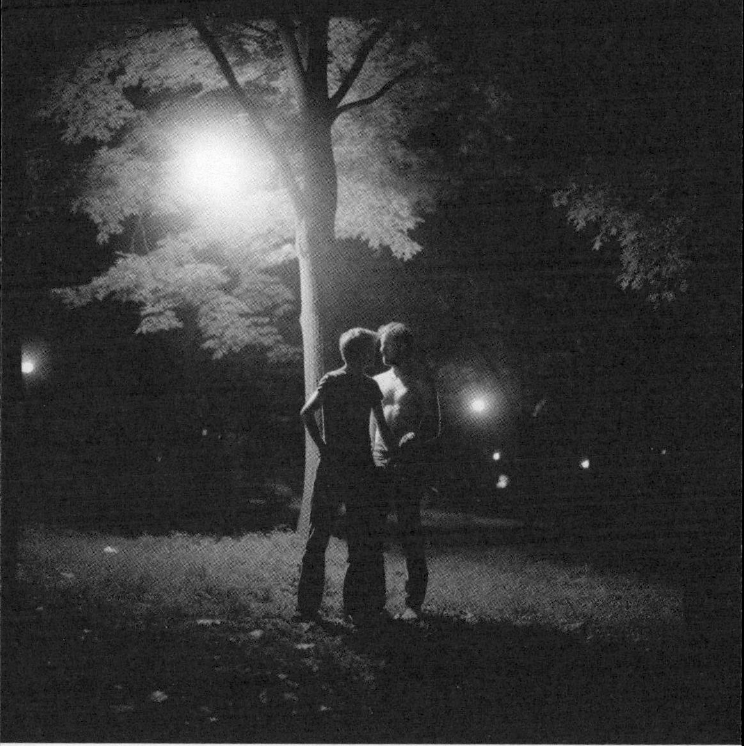

Lots of pigs after 11 pm

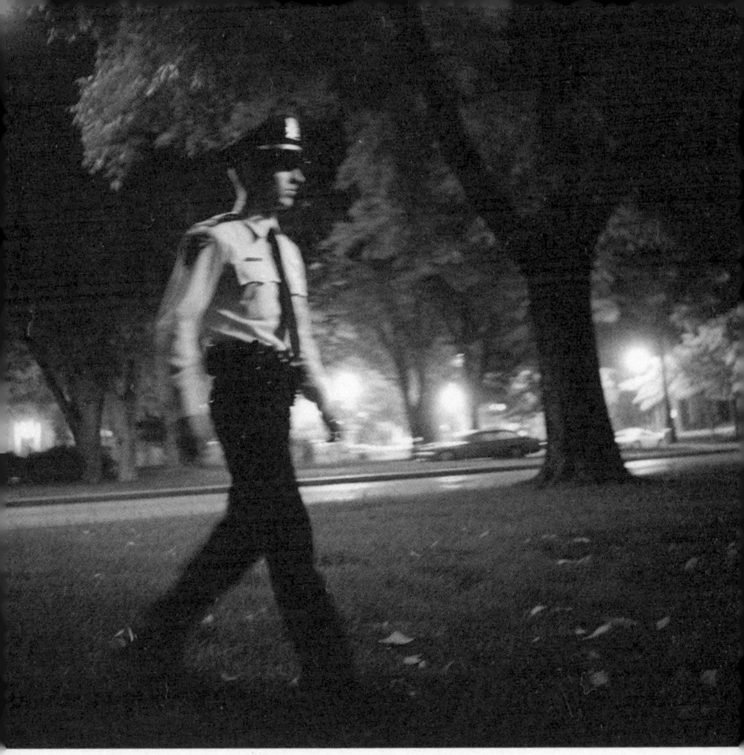

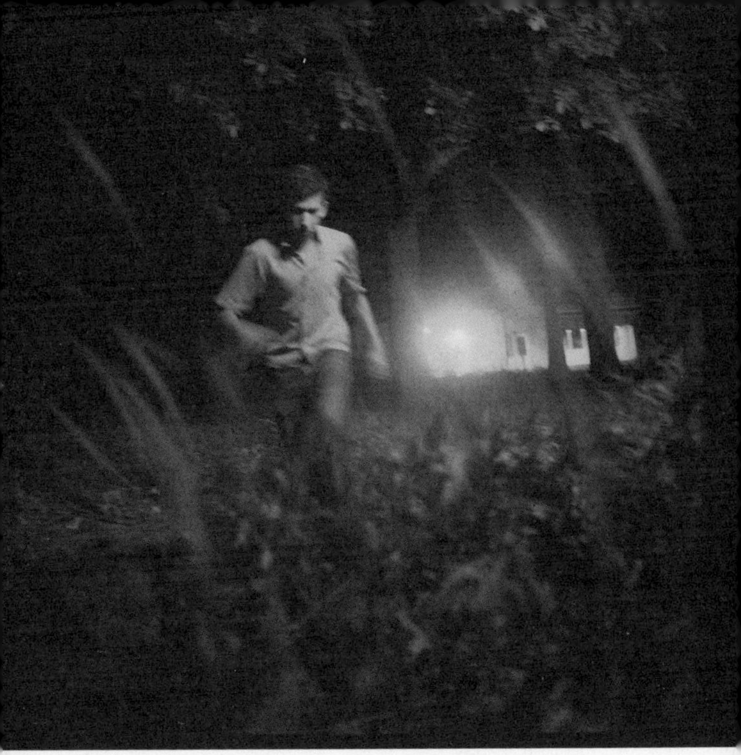

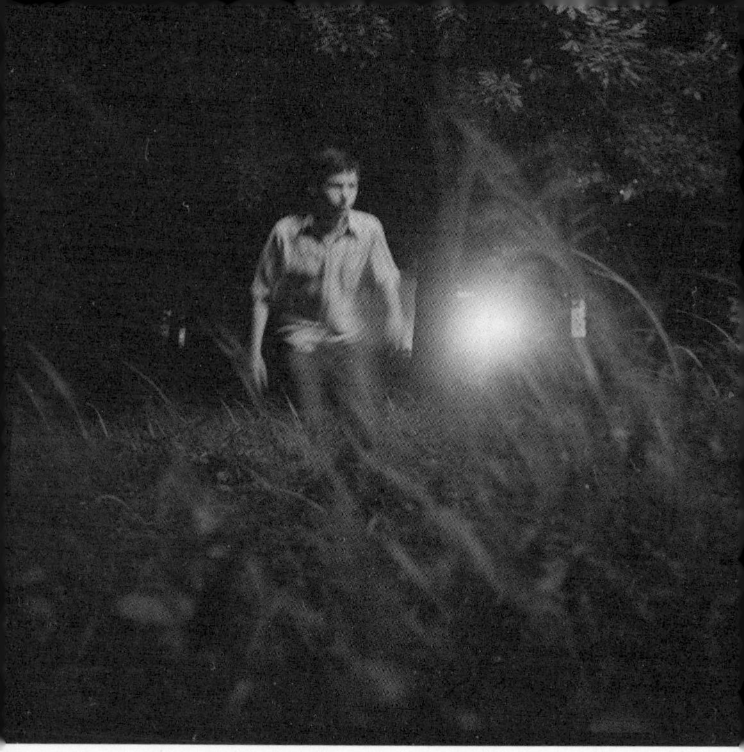

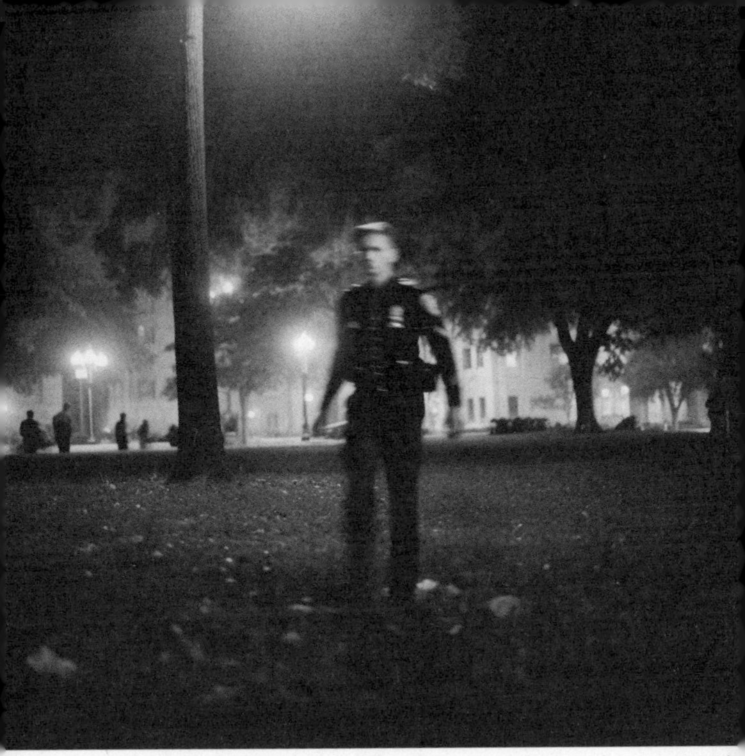

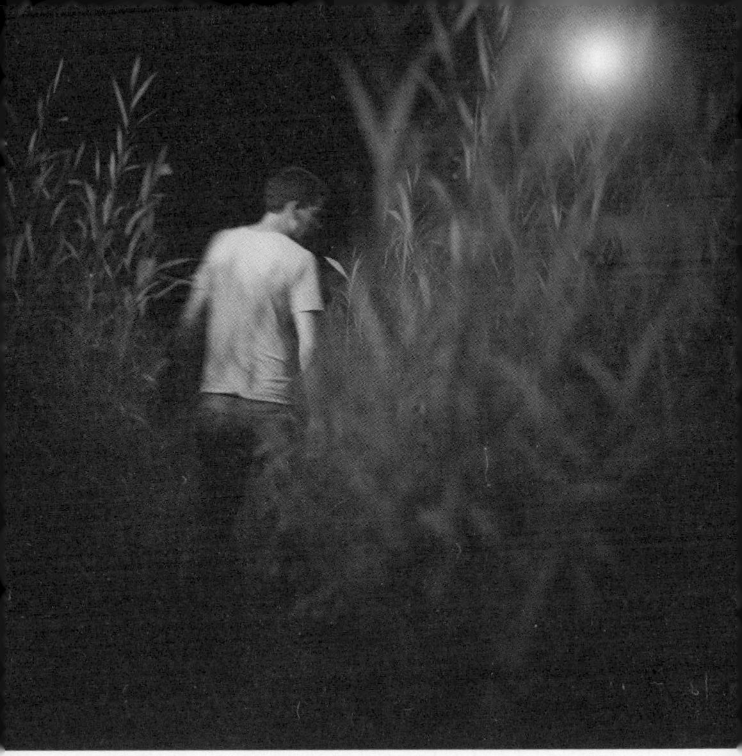

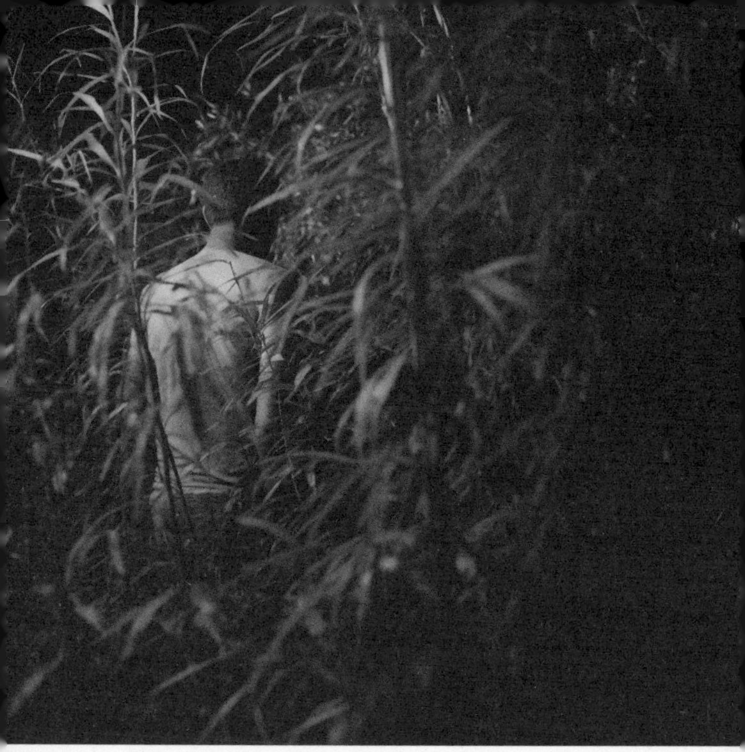

Bring your ID and some cash in case you need to bribe one. A blow job might work as well.

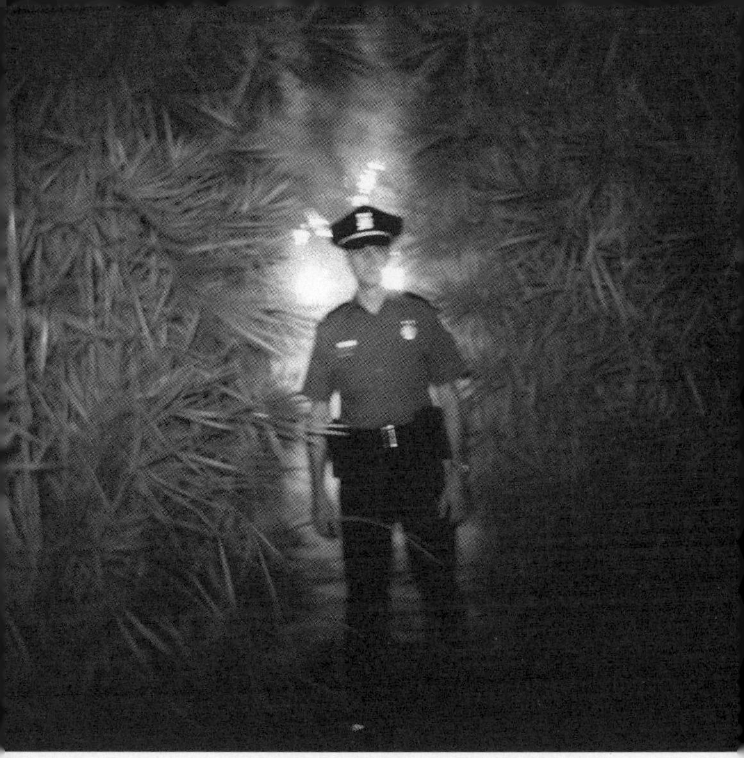

Eye contact is everything. Be bold and don't look away.

If the other guy meets your gaze, that's something. If he nods, that's the green light.

Options include fucking, sucking, jerking.

08. Lavalle VIP Cyber

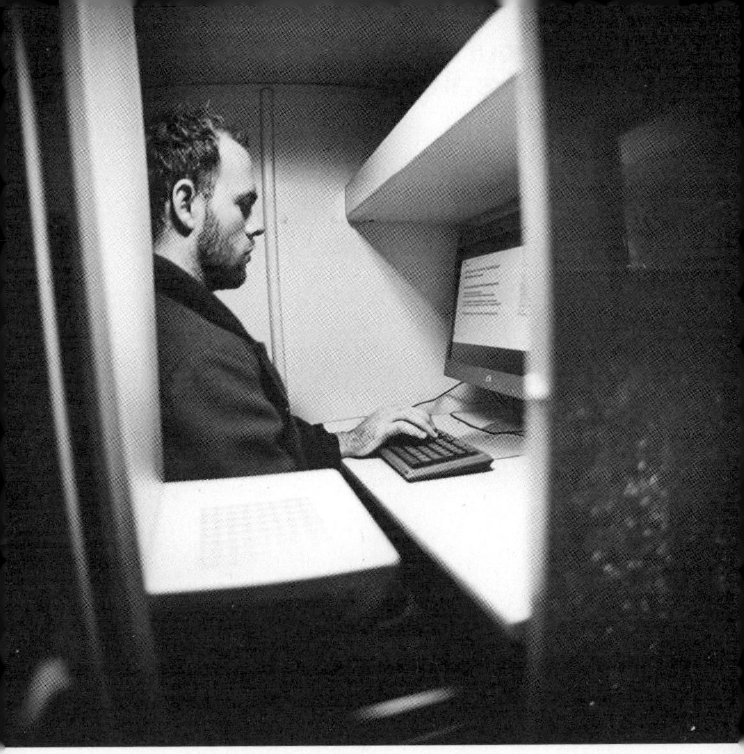

There are about 30 booths. The computers are ancient, but funtional.

You ask for a computer at the entrance and they give you the key to your booth.

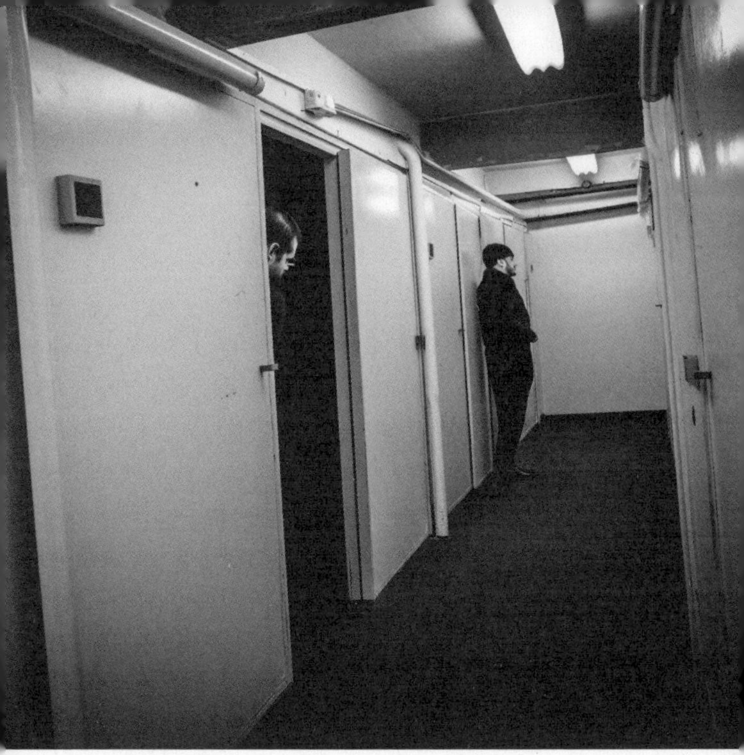

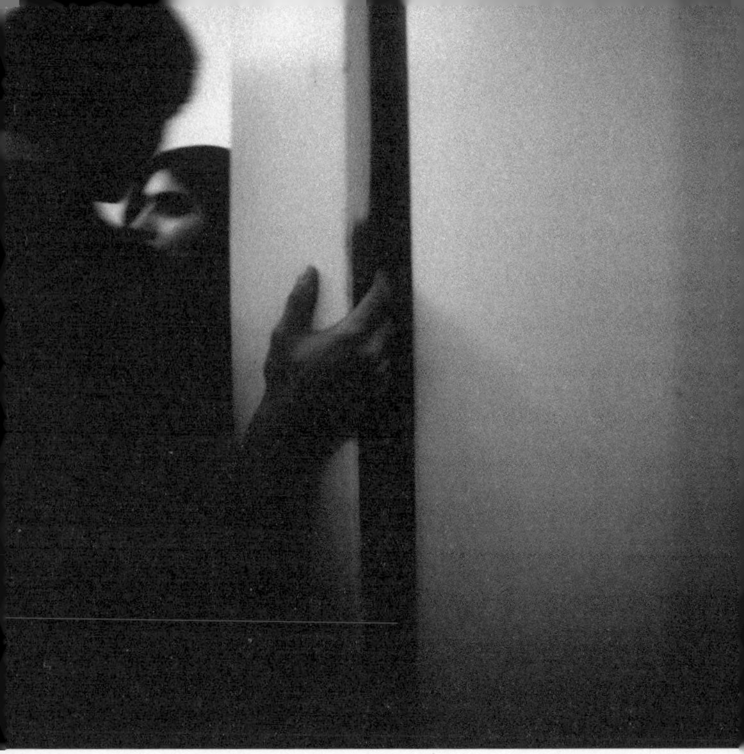

The crowd can be hit-or- miss. Lots of looking, but no moves.

The service is shit, but if there's nothing else... It's central. The curious guys arrive after 5PM.

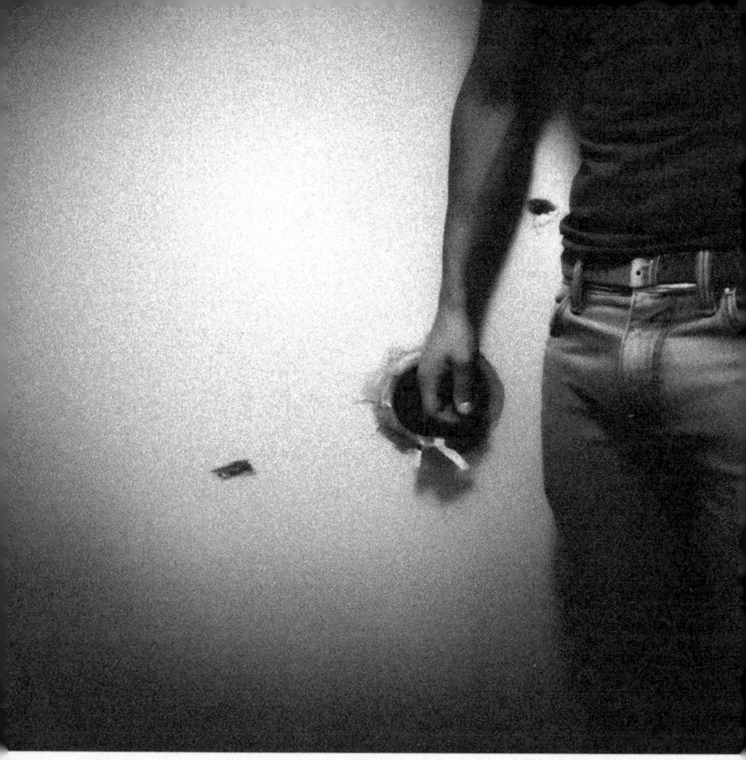

Gestures are basic and don't need much explanation: a head nod, hand movements that mimic jerking-off, etc, etc.

Some show their dicks right away. Usually hung tops who want to fuck you (at least from my experience).

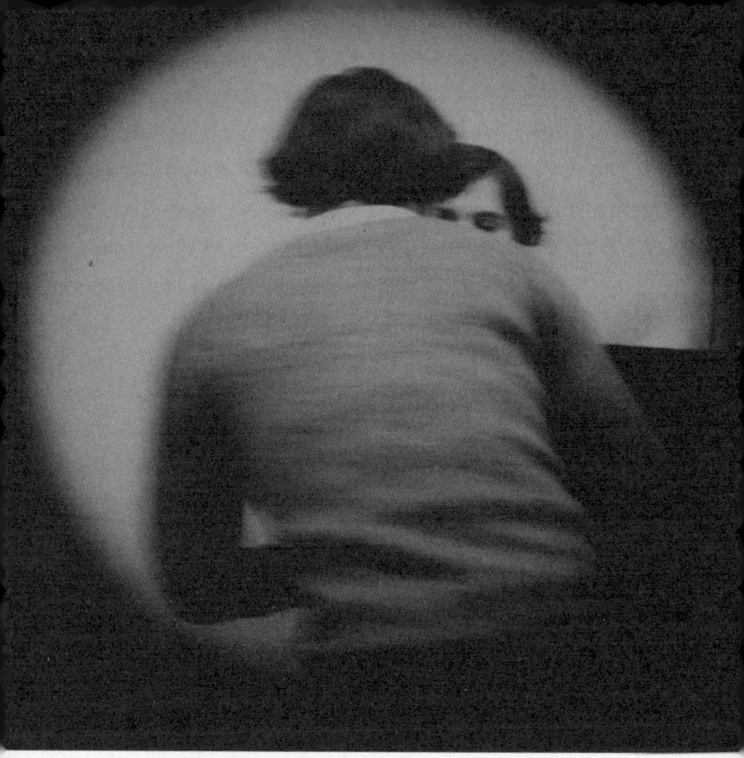

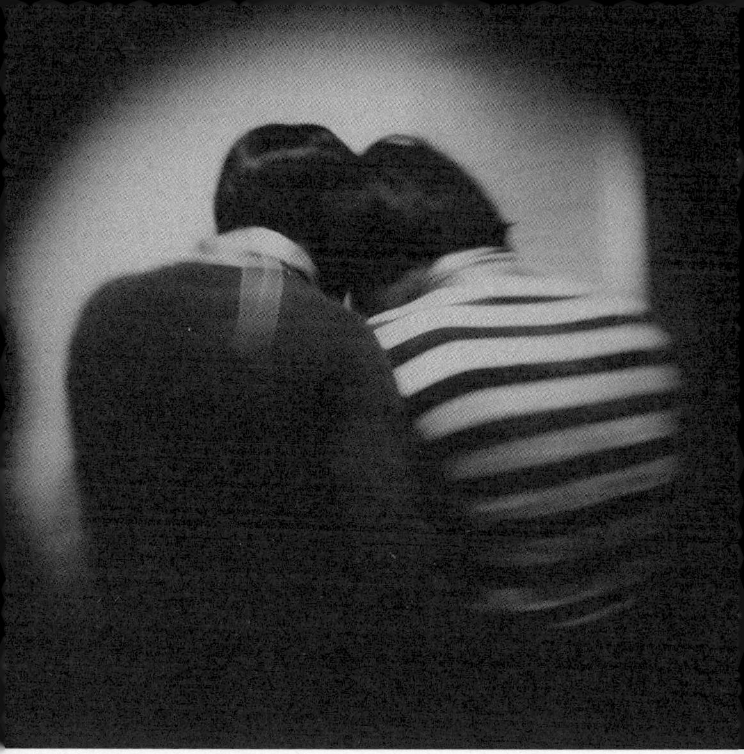

The four booths at the back have glory holes. Everyone wants one.

Once you're in, just move the desk and there you go.

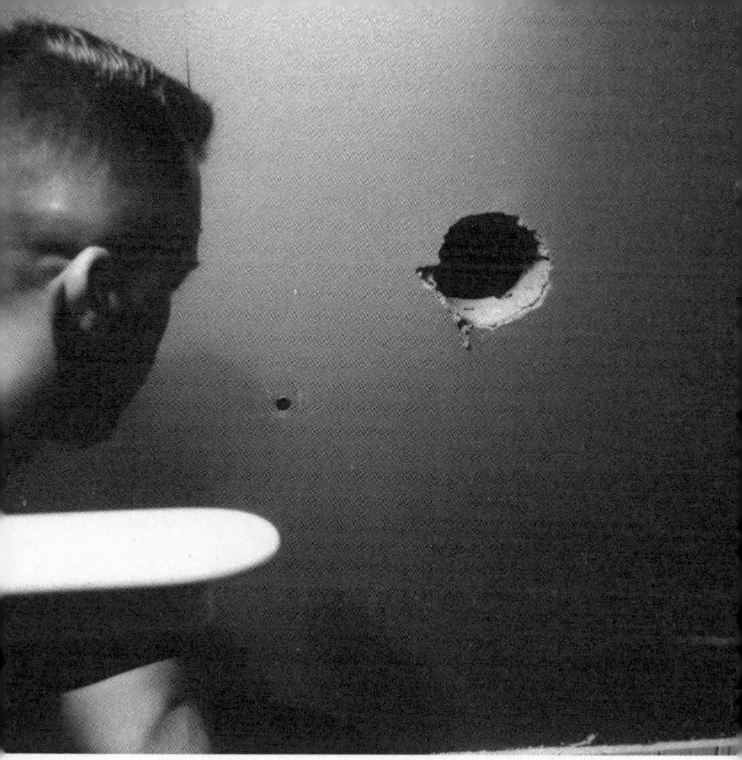

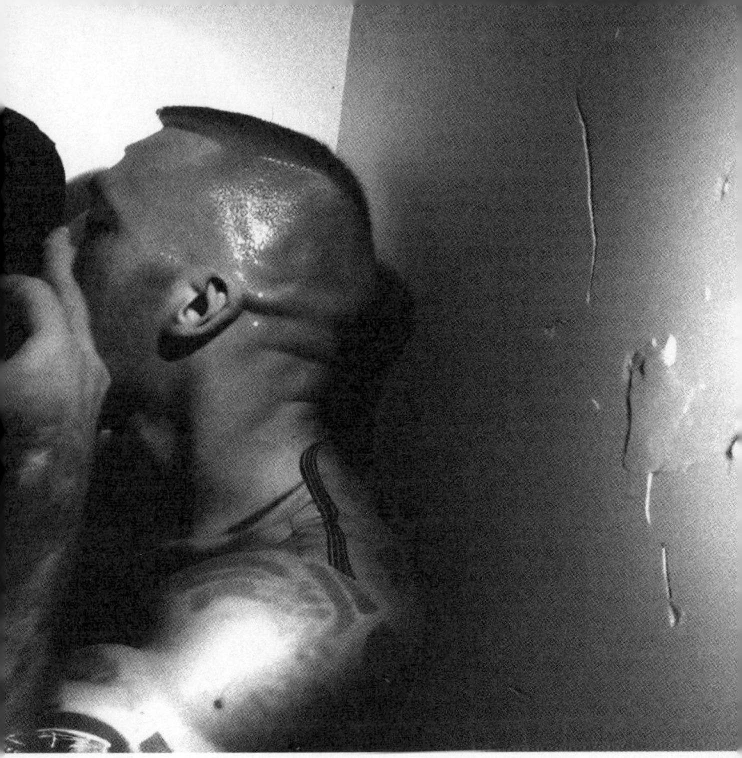

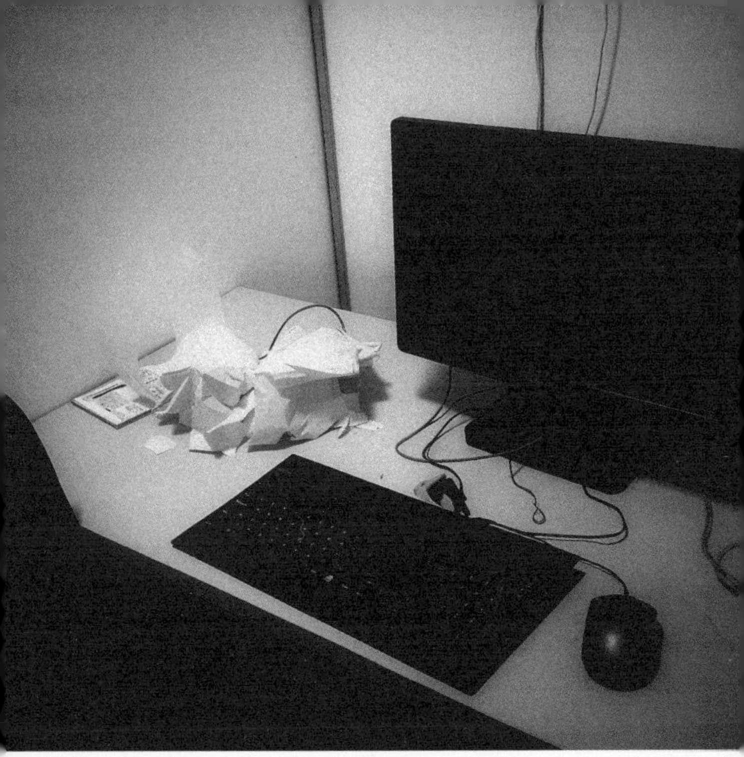

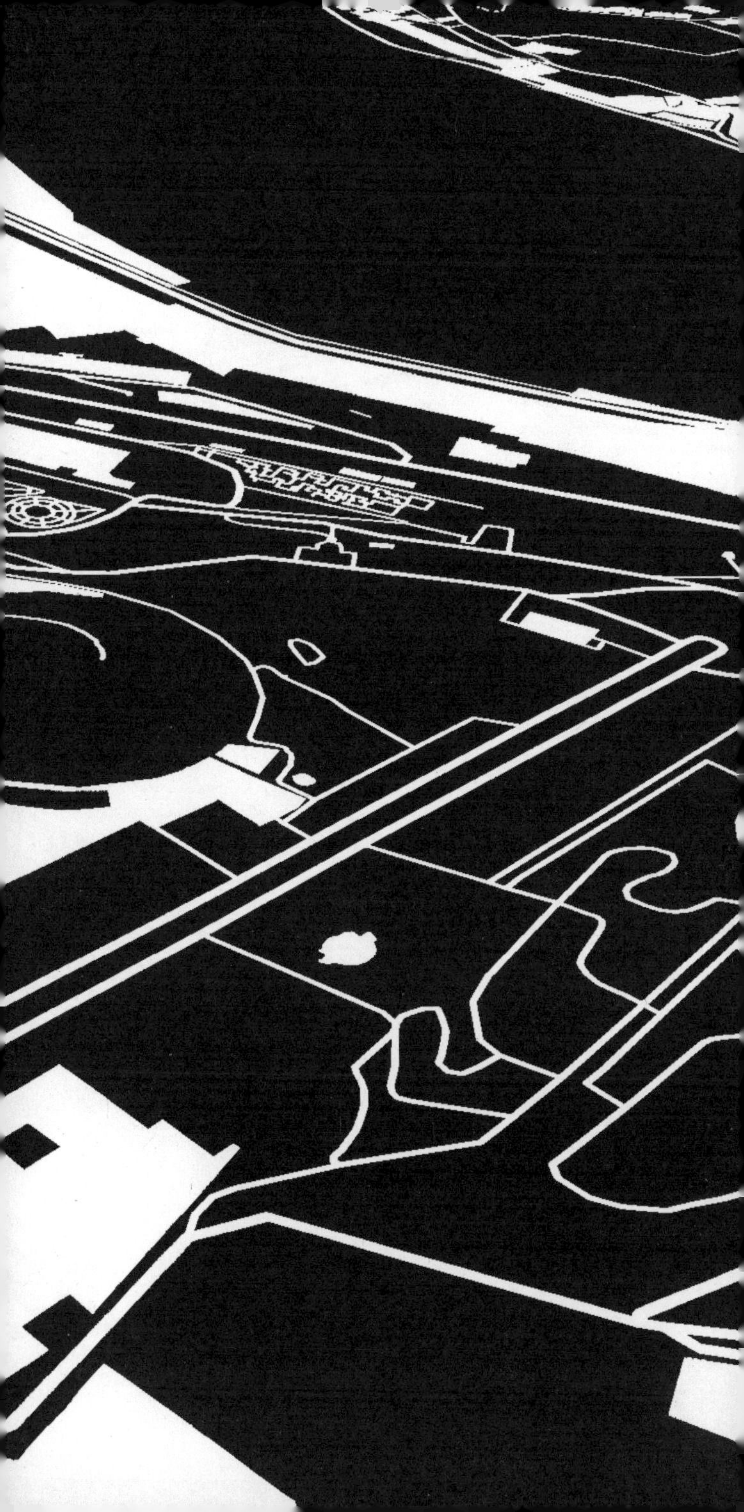

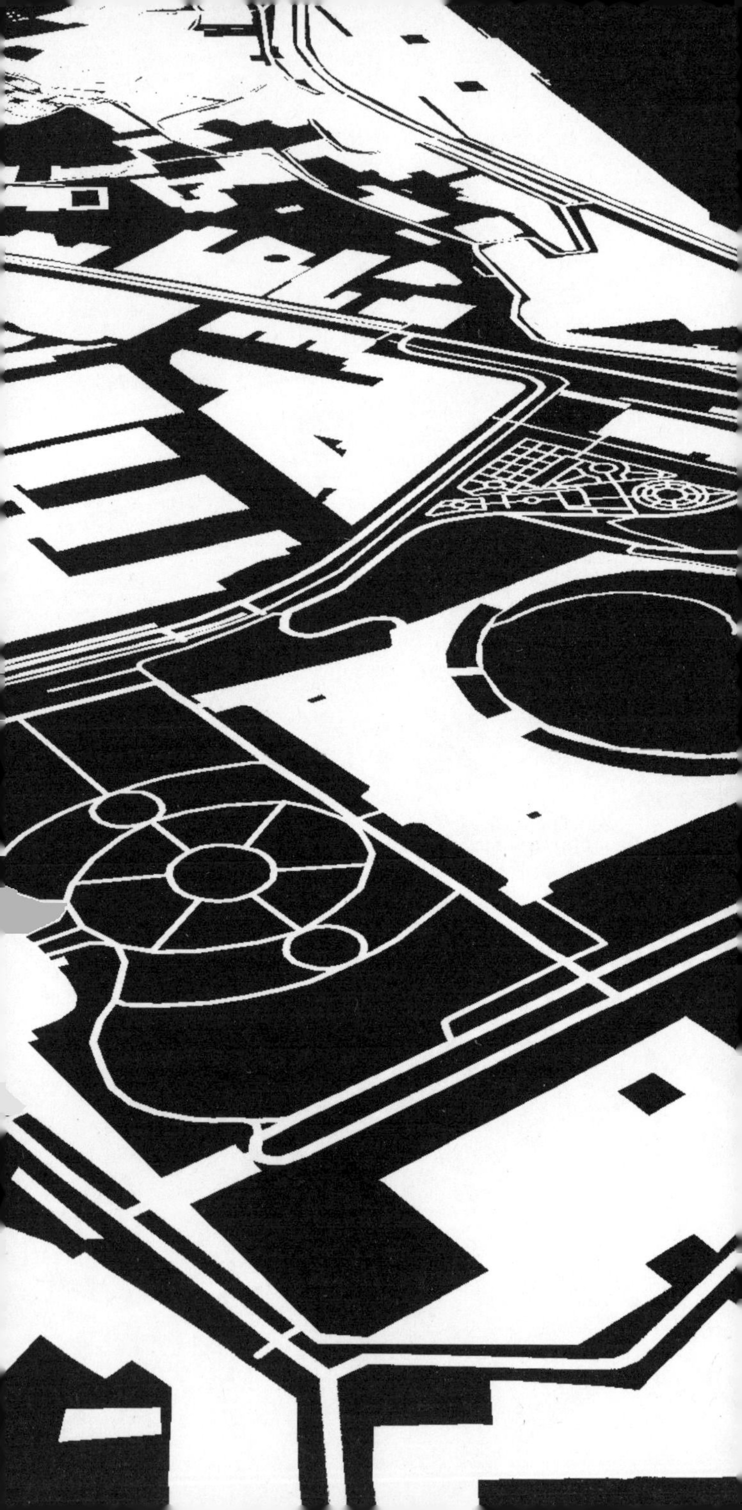

09. Madison Spa

10. ABC Cinema

09. Madison Spa

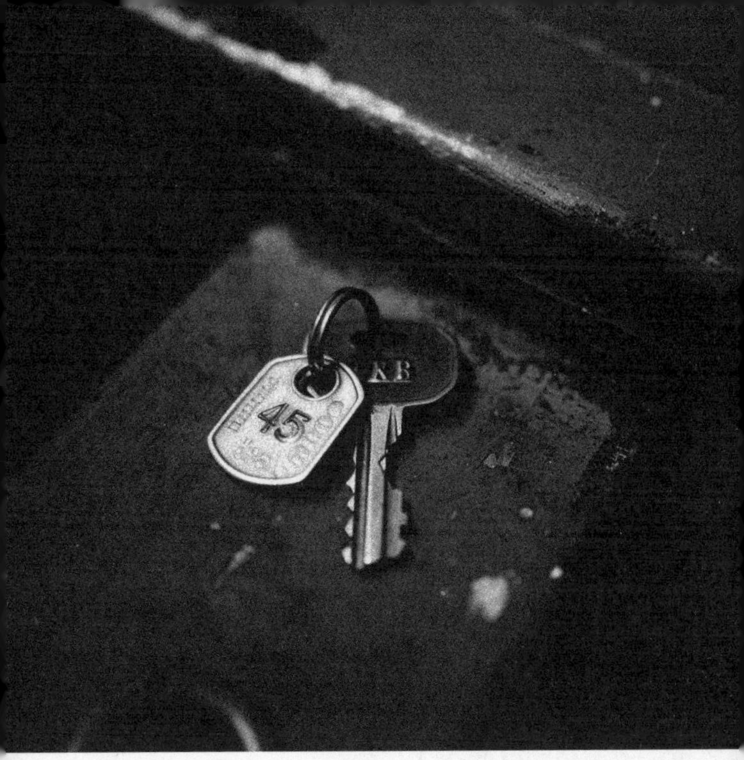
KB
45

Classic cruising spot.

For $350 they give you a stained towel (you can tell they've been cutting them down because they keep getting smaller) and some flip-flops.

Also includes a locker. Don't lose the key. It'll cost you $500 (you might even get your stuff stolen).

The key has a rubber band, which you can use on your wrist. I like to put it on my ankle, just because I hate the way it sounds when im jerking someone off .

TIP: I bring my own towel and a swimsuit or boxer shorts. Honestly, the place isn't great for sitting around naked anywhere. Your own towel's crucial for after, because they only give you one, and it gets soaked in the 'spa.'

MONDAY TO FRIDAY
FROM 3 PM TO 10 PM
(THE SAUNA SHUTS
OFF AT 9 PM, BUT
STAYS WARM FOR A BIT
LONGER)

WEDNESDAYS, UNDER 27
ONLY

SATURDAY FROM 11 AM
TO 10 PM
PRETTY BUSY IN THE
MORNING—the after-party
crowd.

SUNDAY 11 AM TO 7 PM
(NOT MUCH GOING ON)

GENERAL ENTRY $350
WEDNESDAYS $175

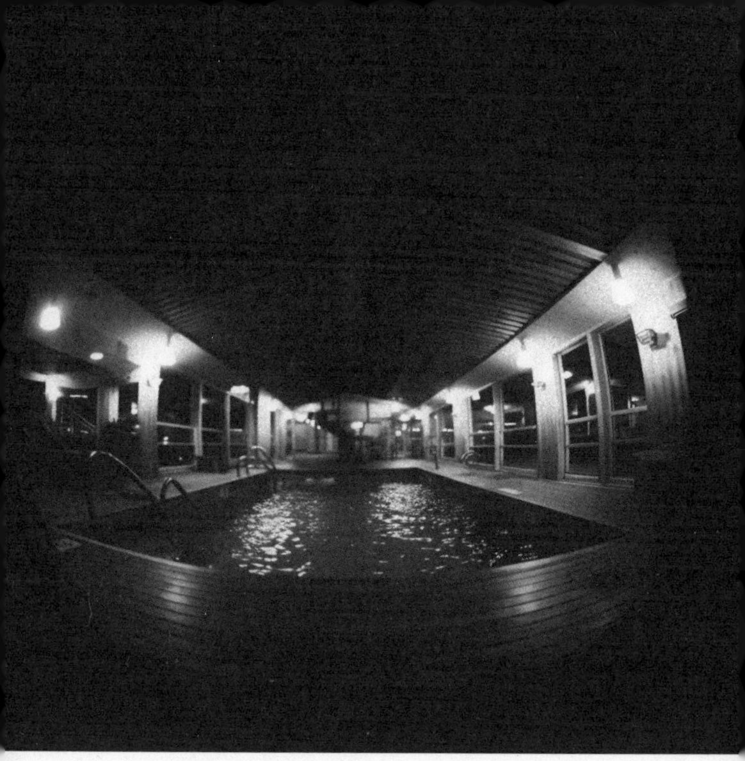

Personally, I find pools pretty gross. Heavy on fucking, light on cleaning. If it's your thing, that's fine. It's shallow and has cool lights.

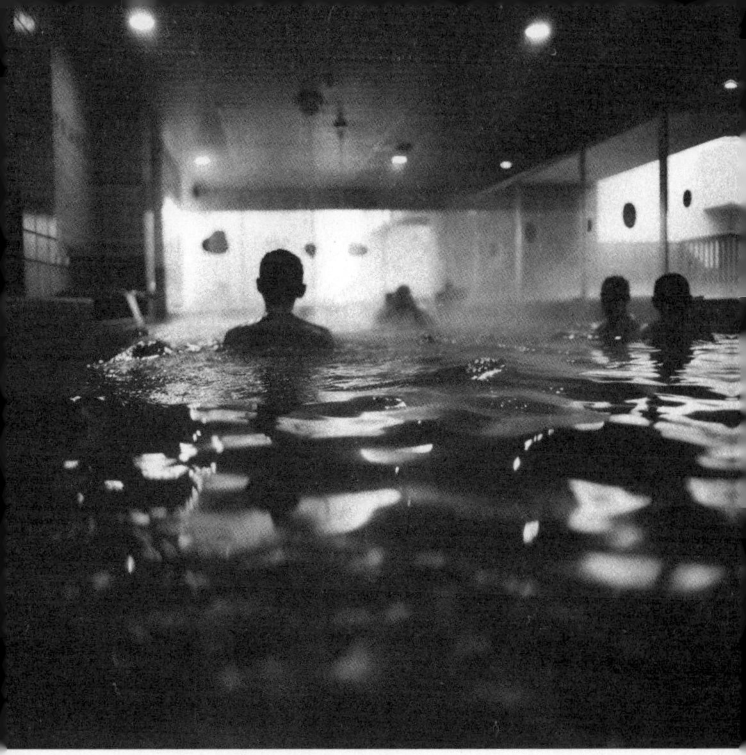

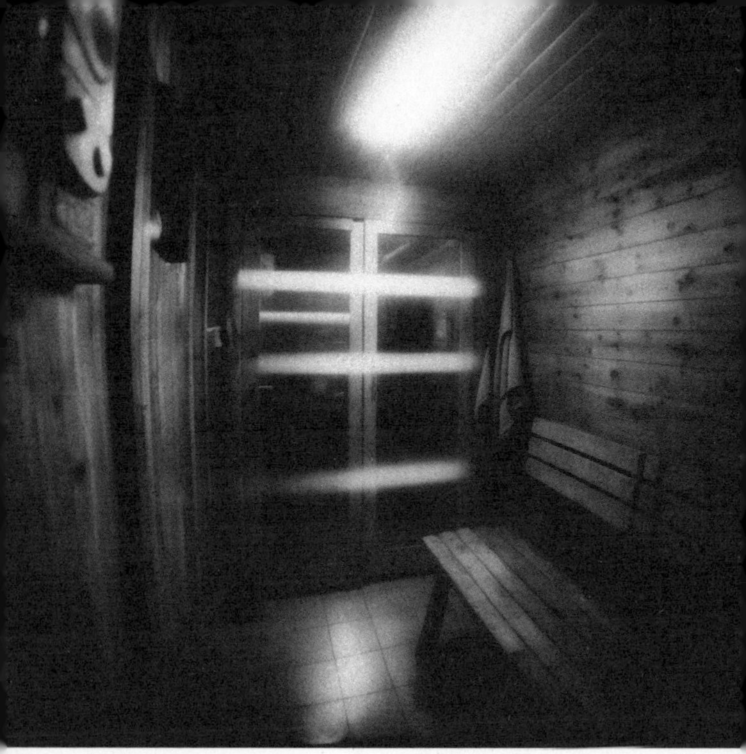

Since the sauna doesn't get too hot, you can stay in for a while. Watch the nails in the wood if you are gonna sit down there. The place needs urgent maintenance.

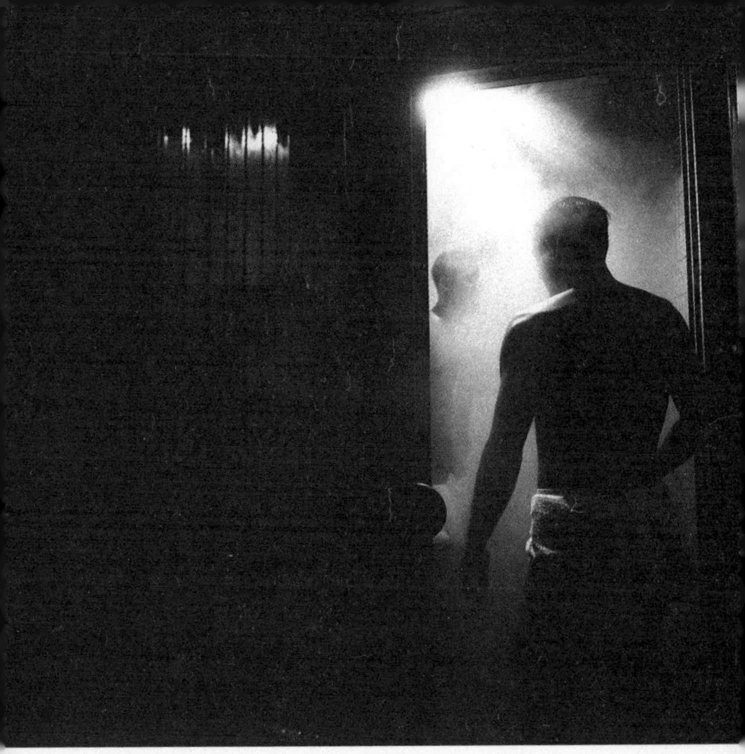

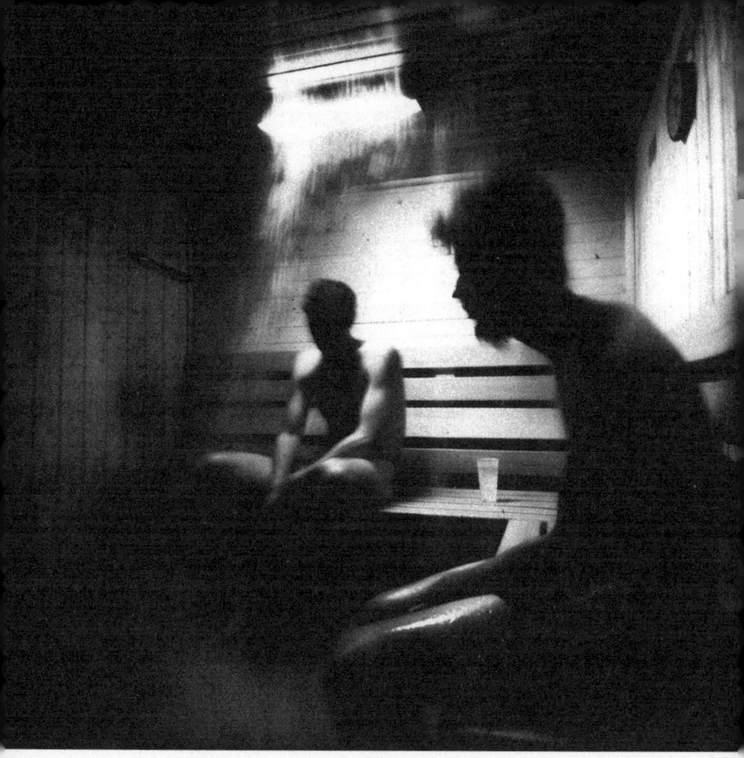

Wednesdays at Madison is 'twink day' Only those under 25 can get in. The admission is half price, and honestly, the crowd is hot.

I know the guy at the entrance and he always lets me in. Looking young helps.

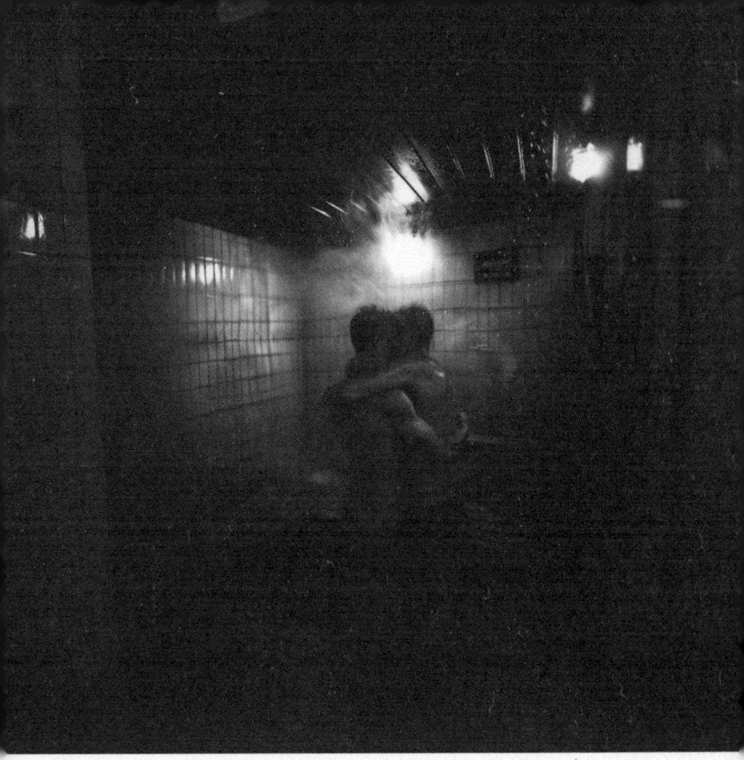

There's a jacuzzi in the basement, which serves as the dark room. Everyone hangs out here even though it smells damp, and you can't hear the music coming from upstairs.

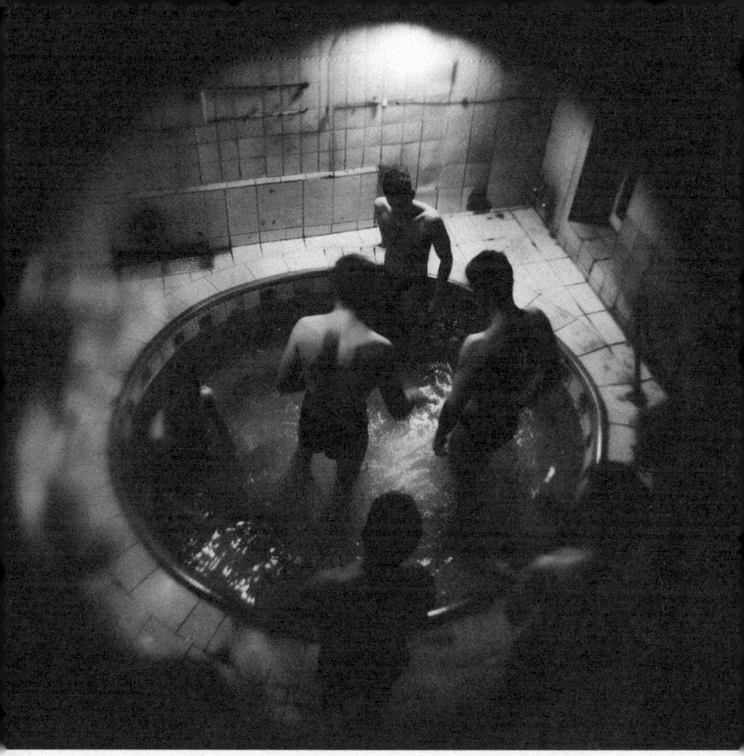

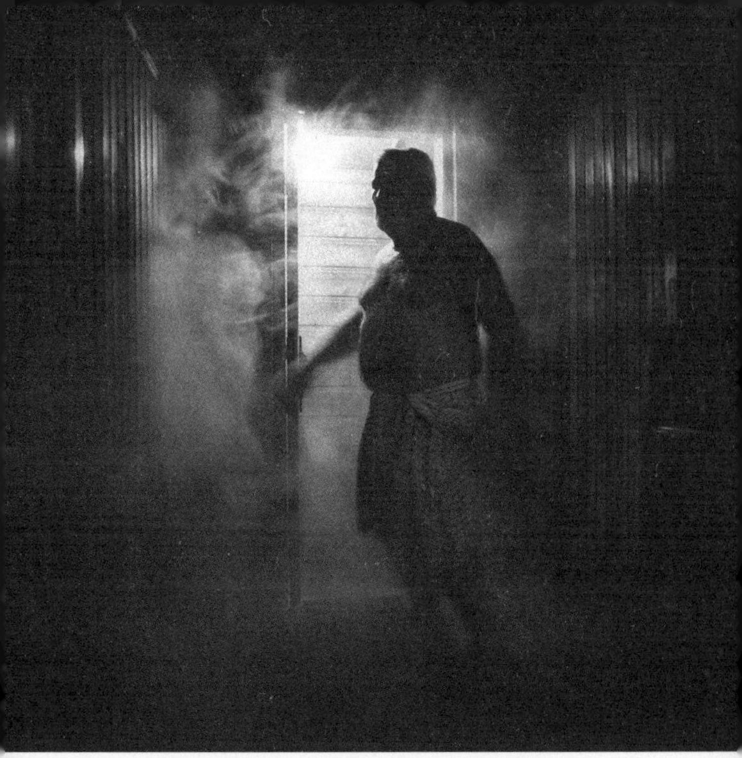

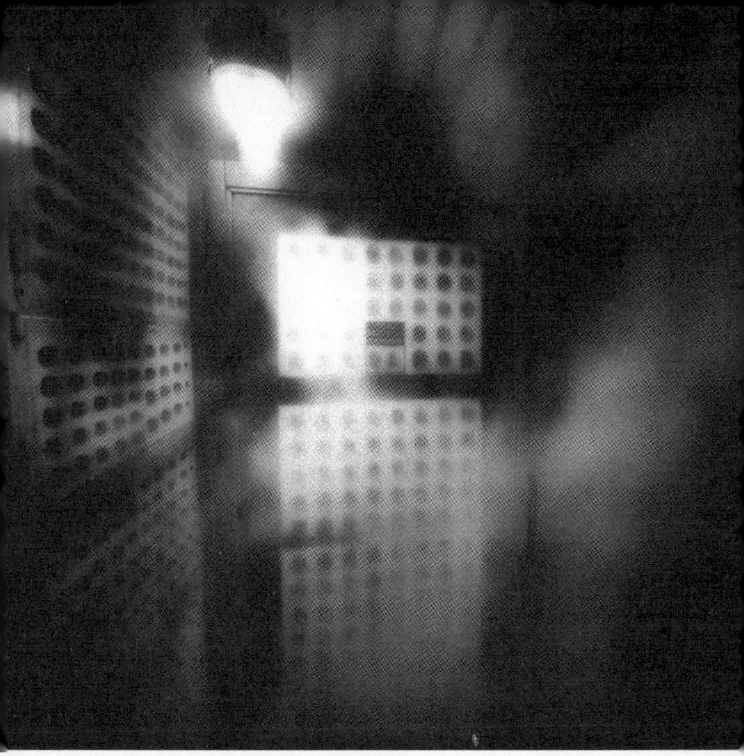

10. ABC Cinema

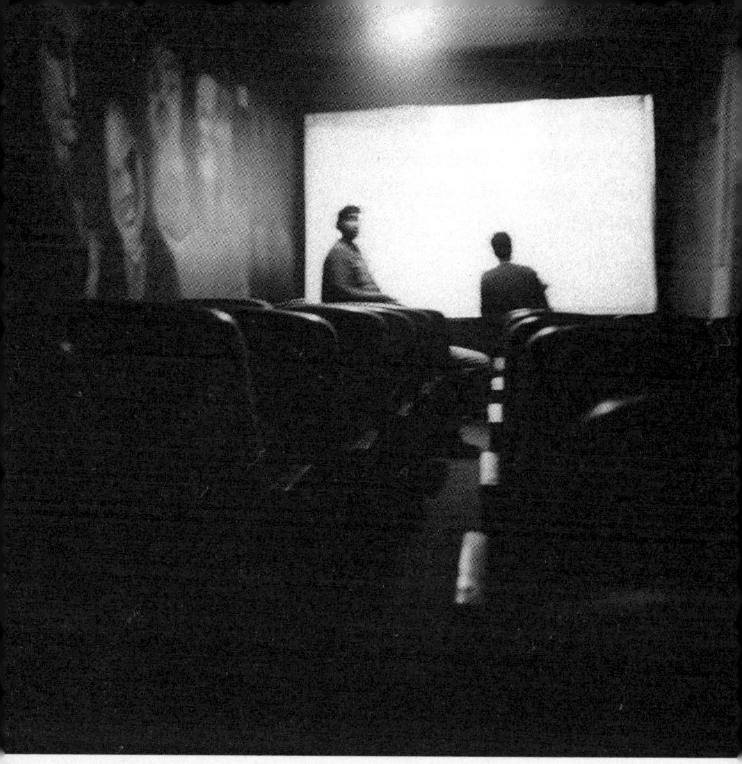

There are five screens—four for straights ones and just one for gays. There's action everywhere, especially upstairs on the balconies.

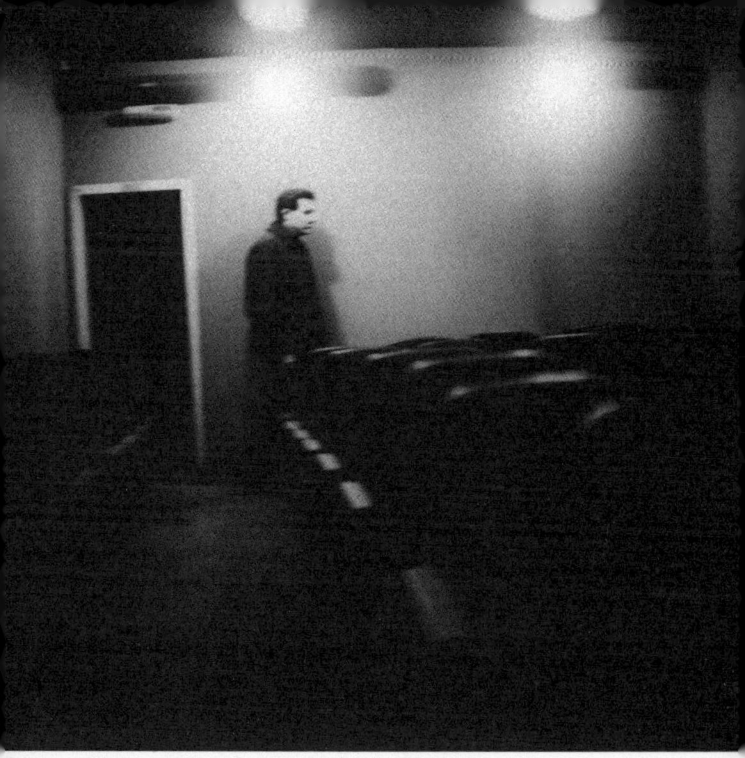

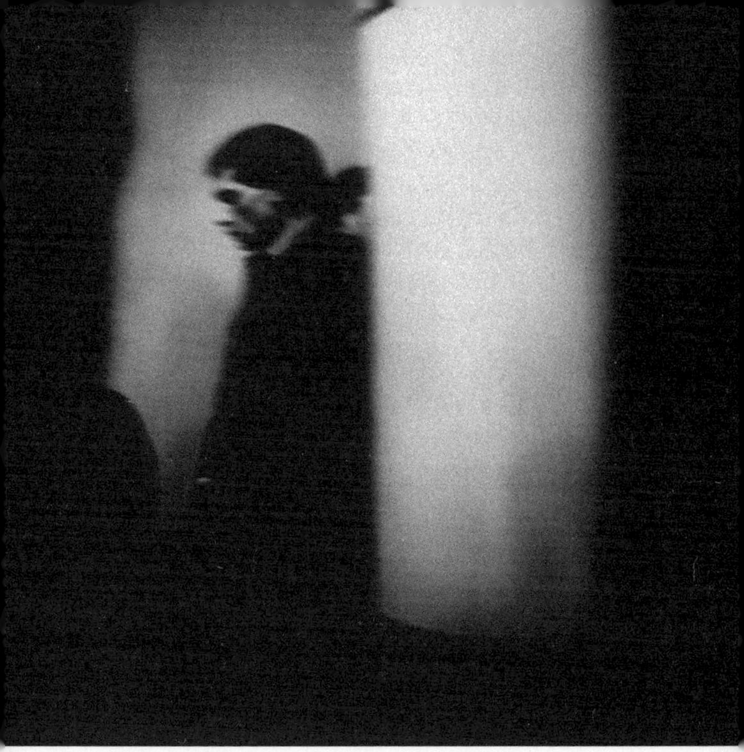

One of the oldest porno theaters in town. True to its name, a good spot for newcomers. It's kept that retro vibe specially at the entrance and ticket booth. It's been around for over 70 years, but started off screening different types of movies.

No backpacks allowed—you gotta check them for $50. Don't bring anything valuable.

After all those years, a lot has gone to shit. Most of the rooms have busted speakers. It's can be a little weird to give a blow job in total silence, but you get used to it.

ABC is light on supplies, so make sure to bring napkins, Restrooms have gloryholes and that's about it.

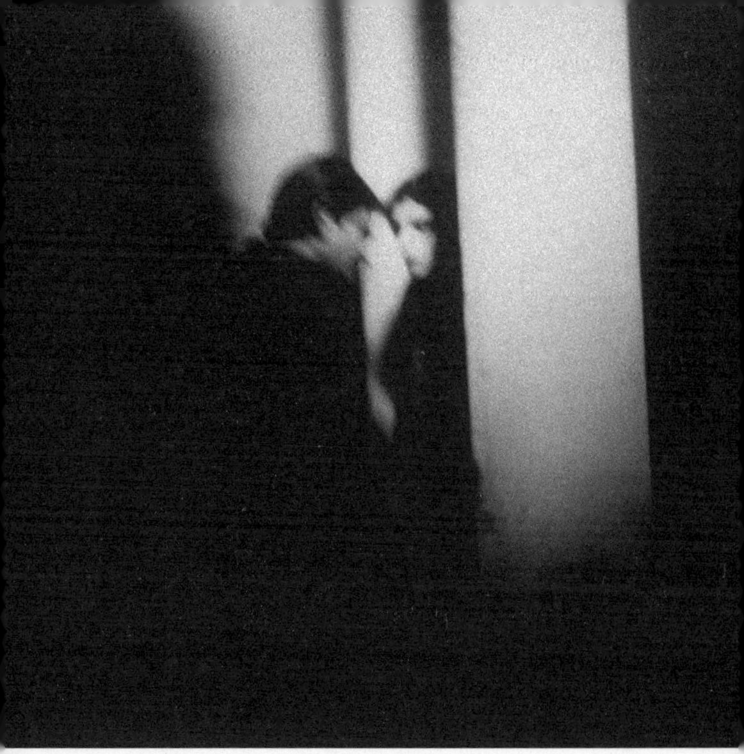

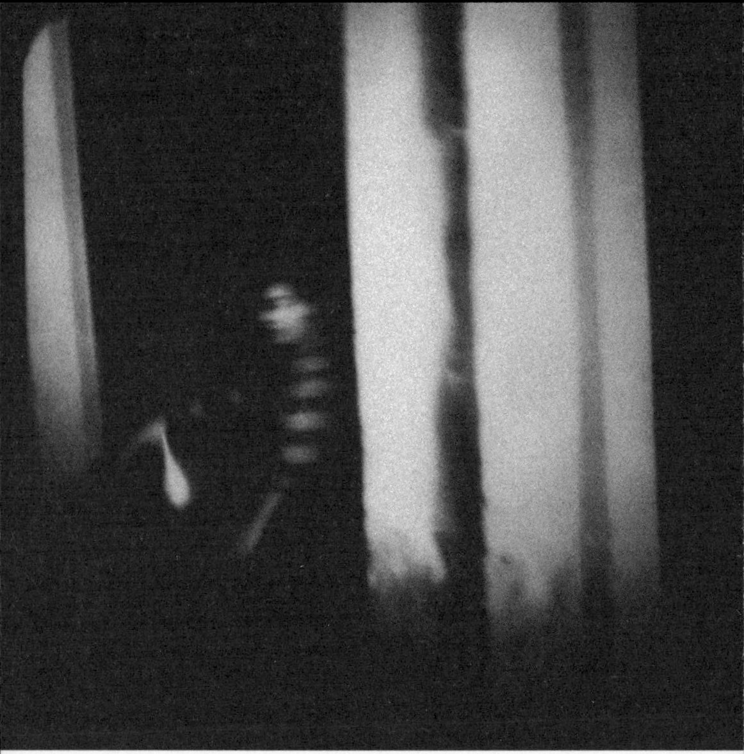

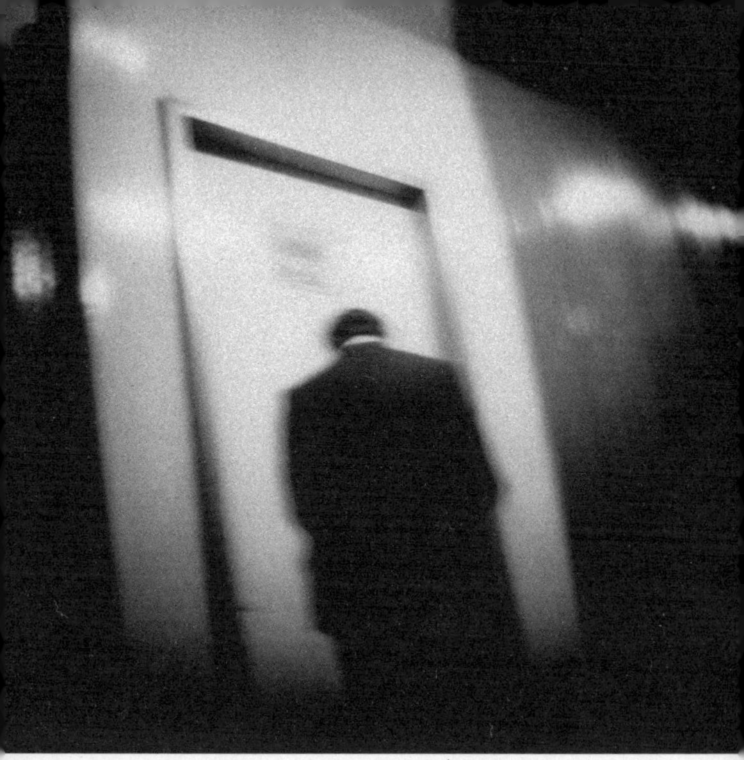

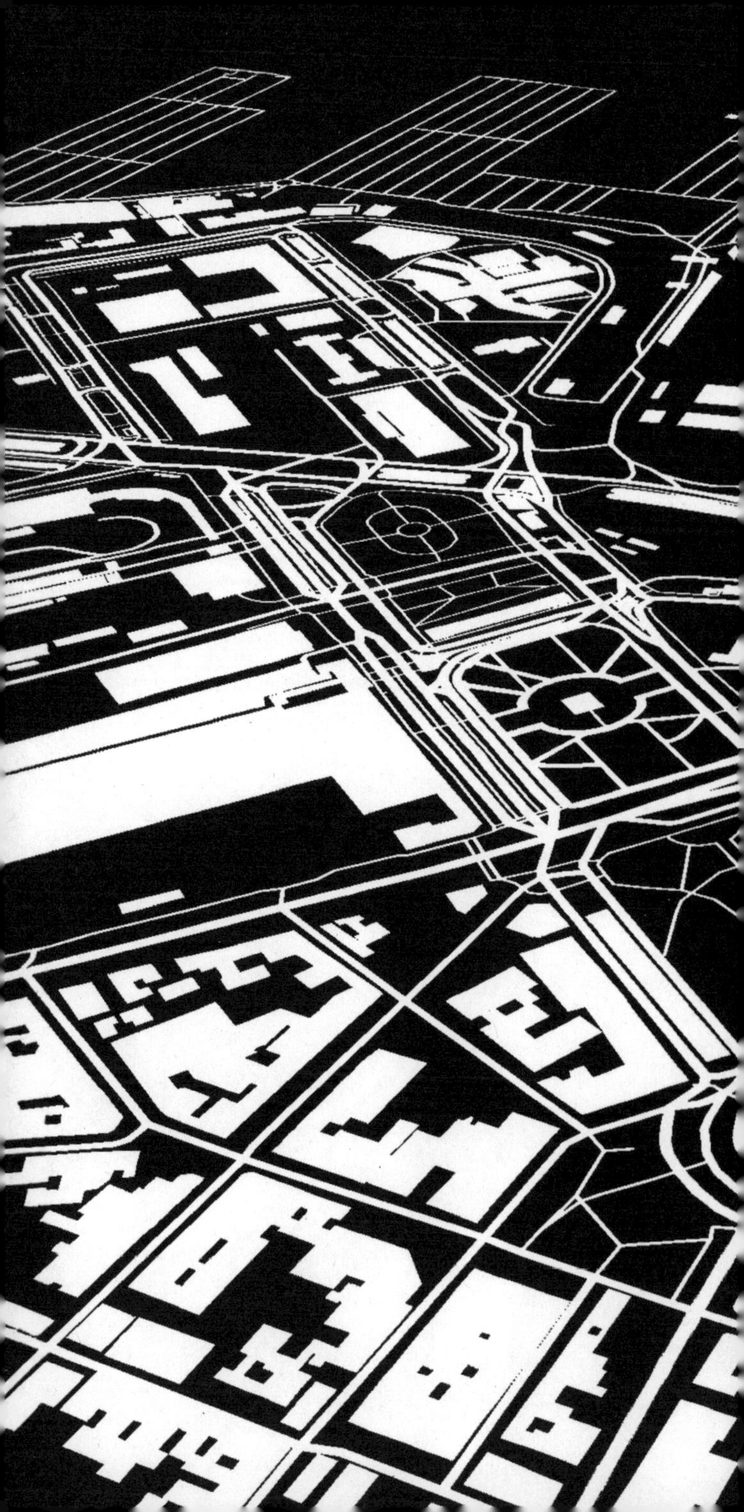

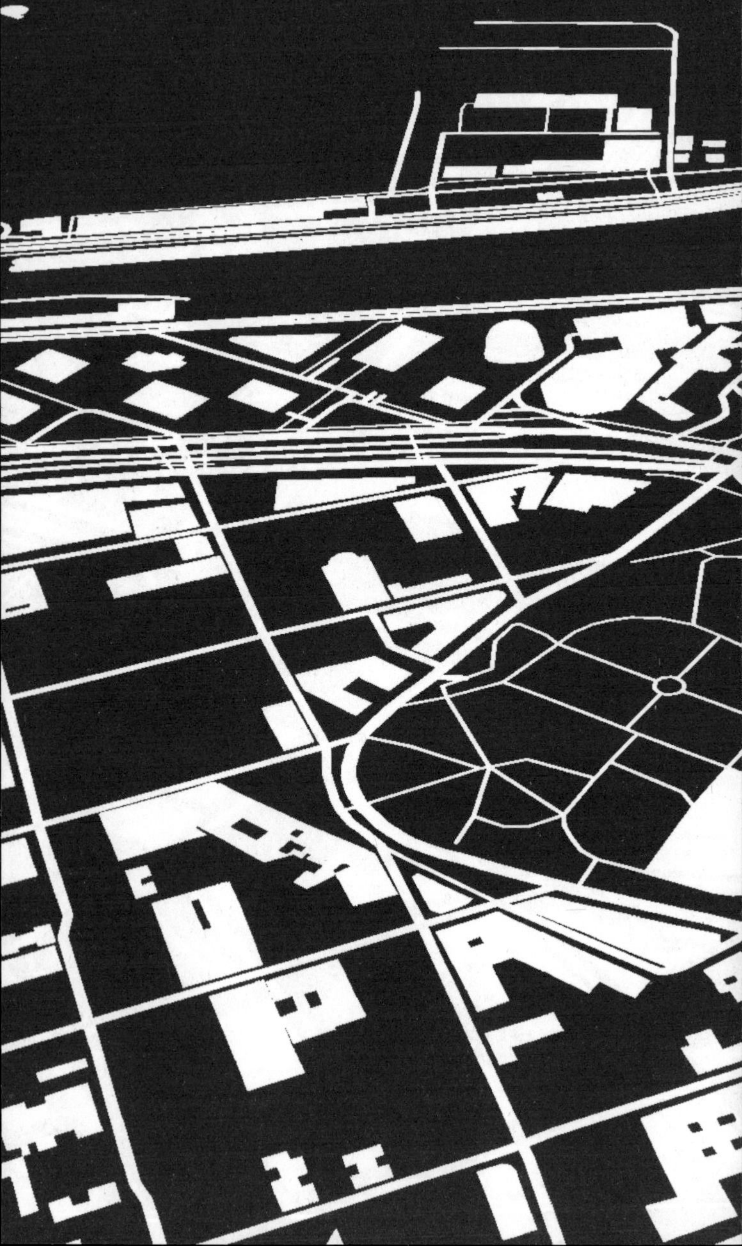

11. The Streets of Lezama Park

12. Walmart Parking Lot

11. The Streets of Lezama Park

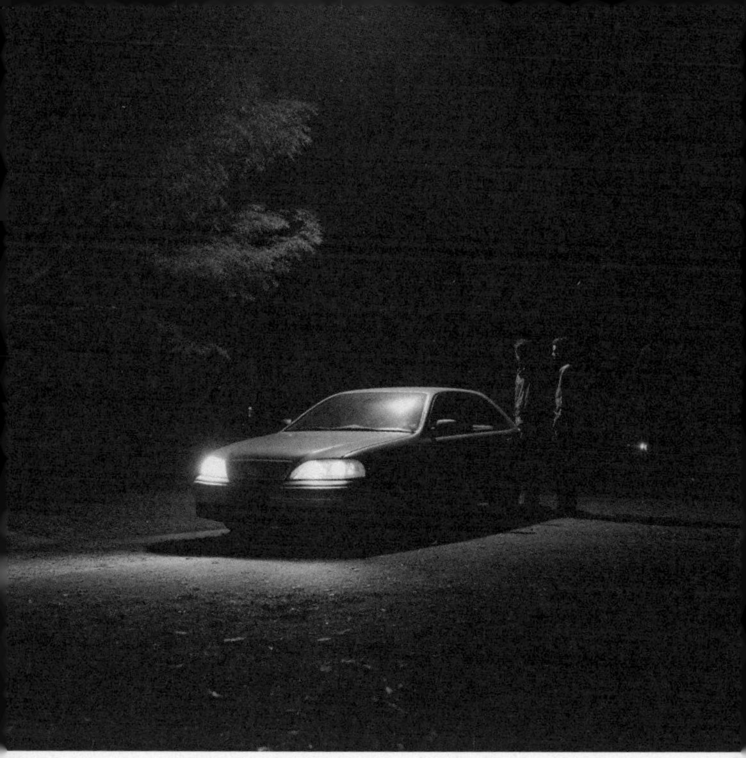

Lakeside street is where the hookers hang. But if you go a little further you'll reach the side streets.
You are sure to find someone who doesn't want go home horny.

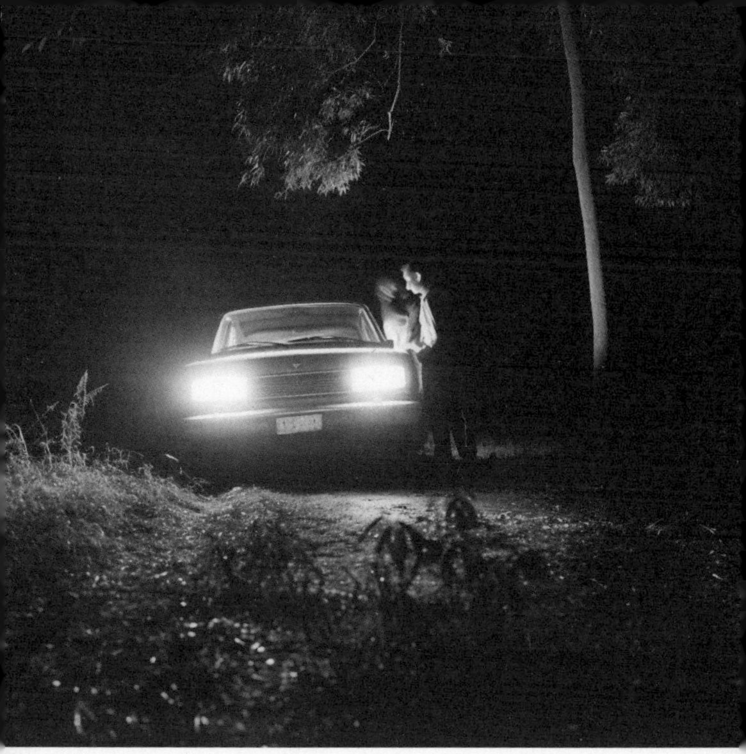

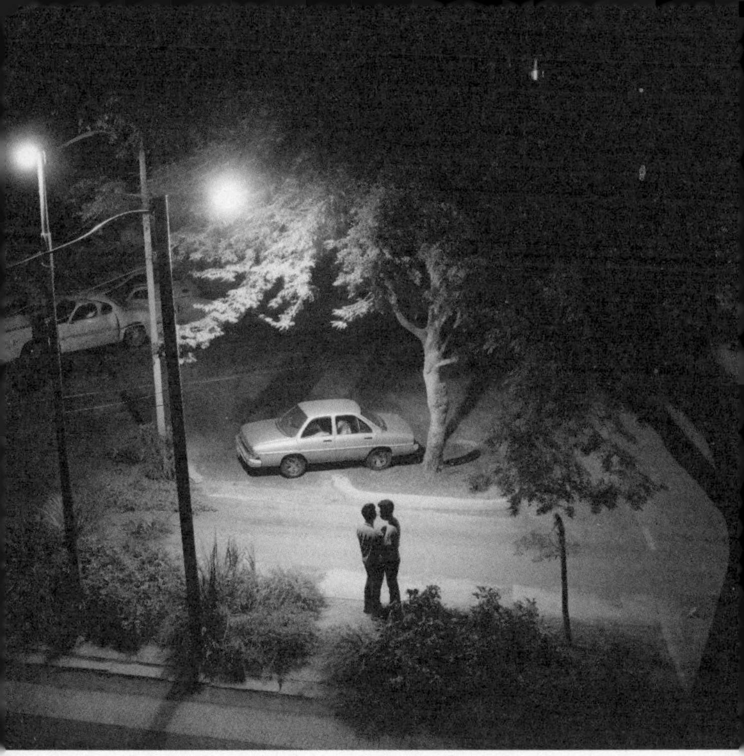

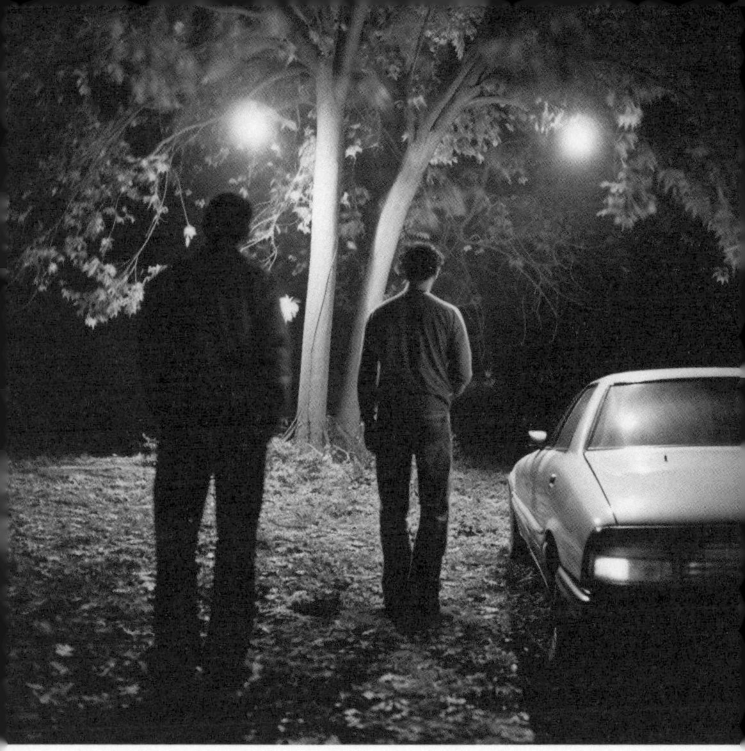

Some dudes park with windows down, inviting you to scope them out, maybe catch a glimpse at their dicks before getting in.

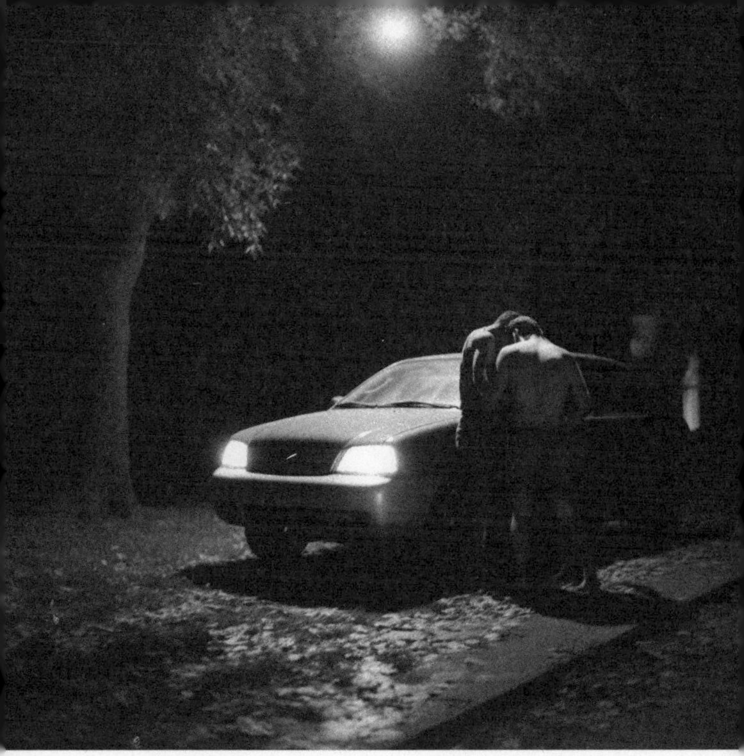

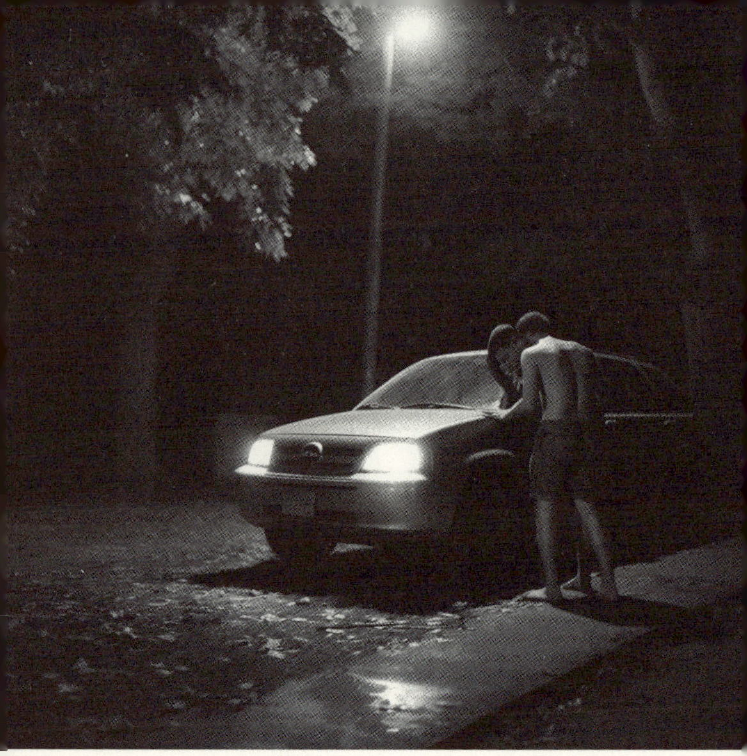

The park is massive, with quiet nooks off the beaten path. Stay low-key, avoid drawing too much attention.

A good spot is near the exercise machines.
The guys working out know there's action in the park, and they might want to get a quick blowjob there.

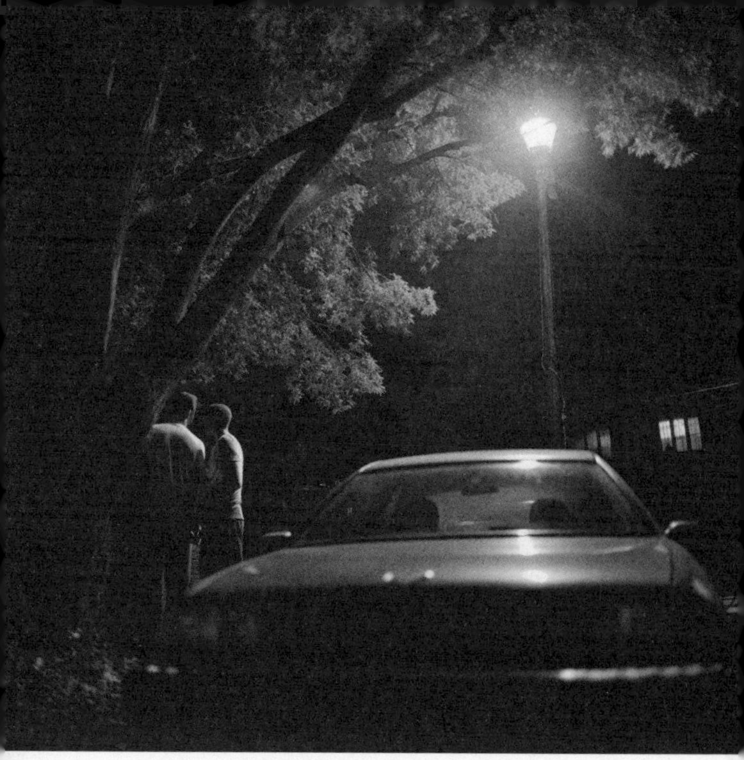

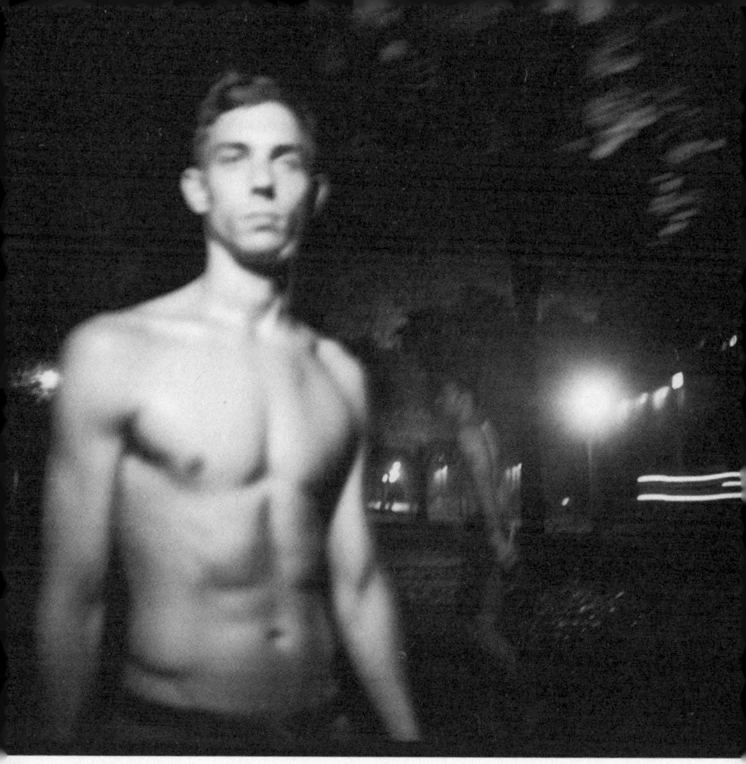

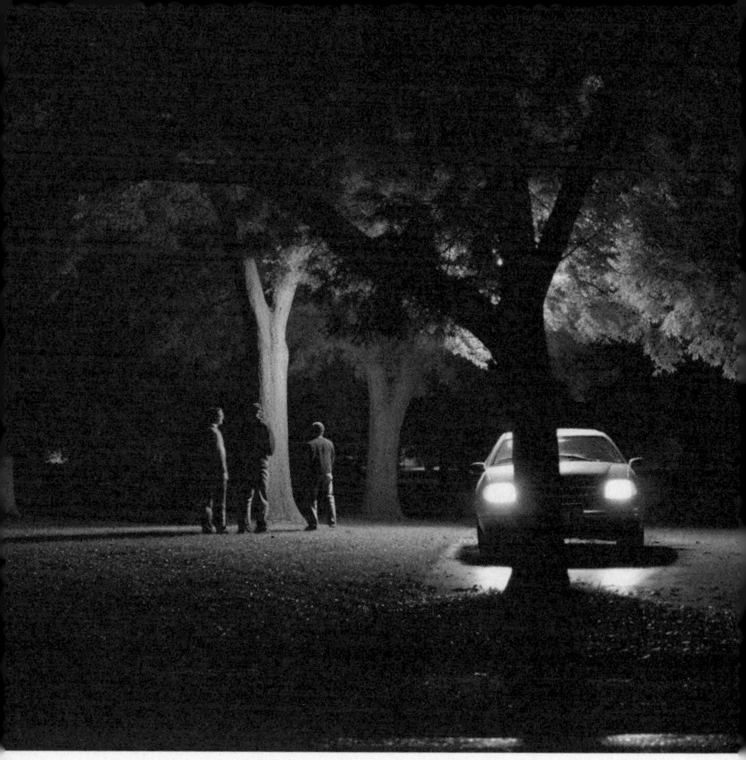

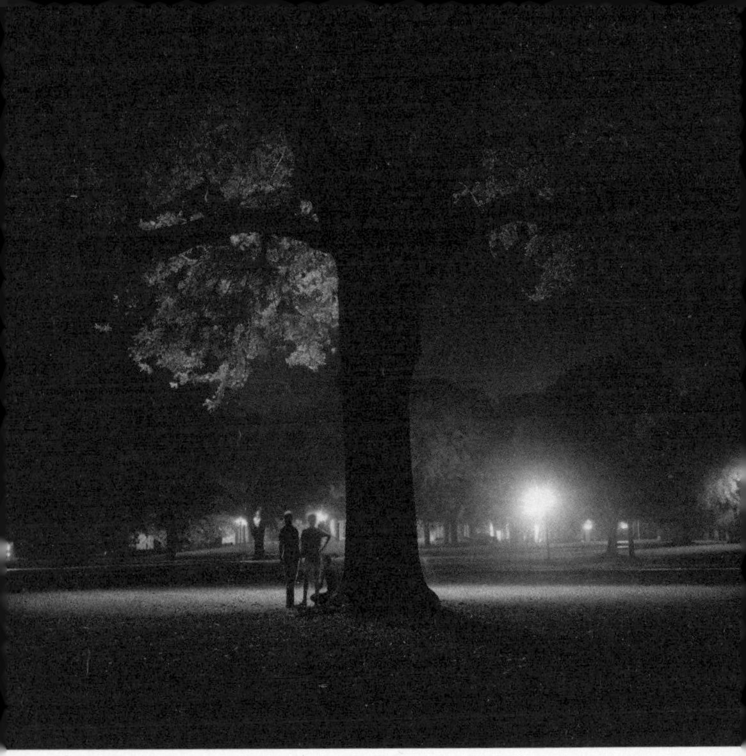

12. Walmart Parking Lot

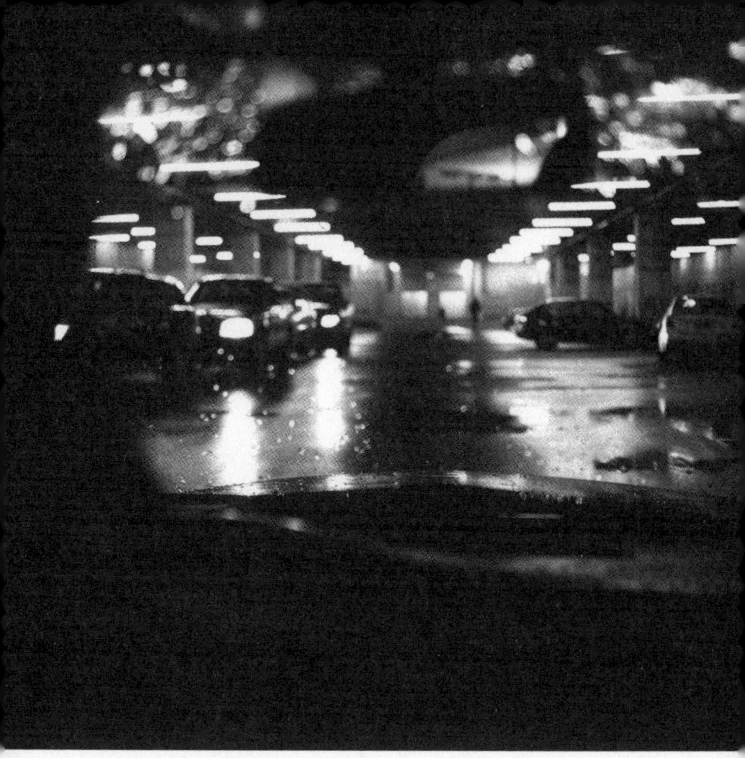

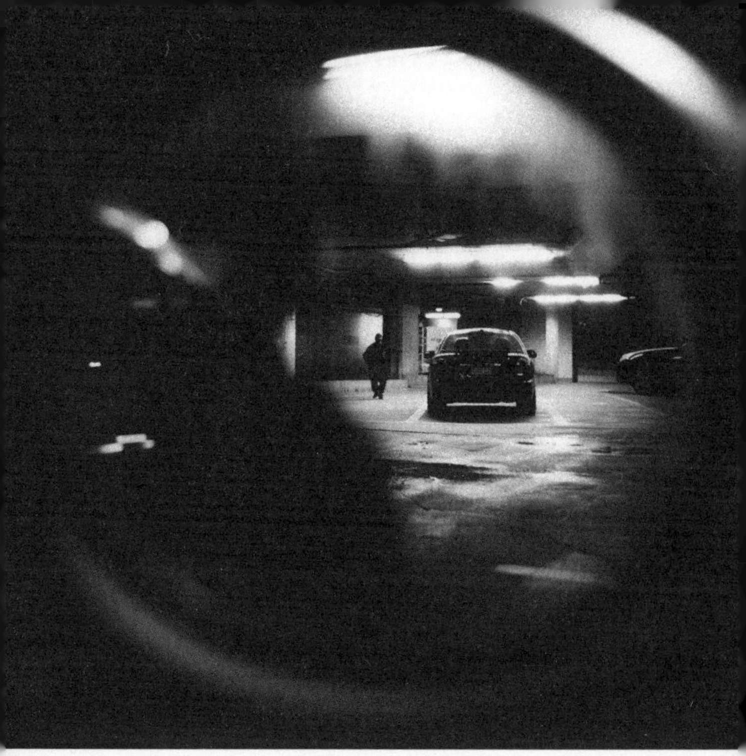

Walmart Parking Lot has been a gay icon since the 2000s when it opened. Now it's become trendy and got quite a bit of exposure on social media, so I'm not sure if it's still the same as it was.

Usually there's plenty of cruising over there. Lots of guys hanging around outside their cars, on their phones, or smoking a cig.

Everyone knows the vibe here.

You've got two options: head to the parking lot bathrooms (they're next to the exit ramp) or get into a car.

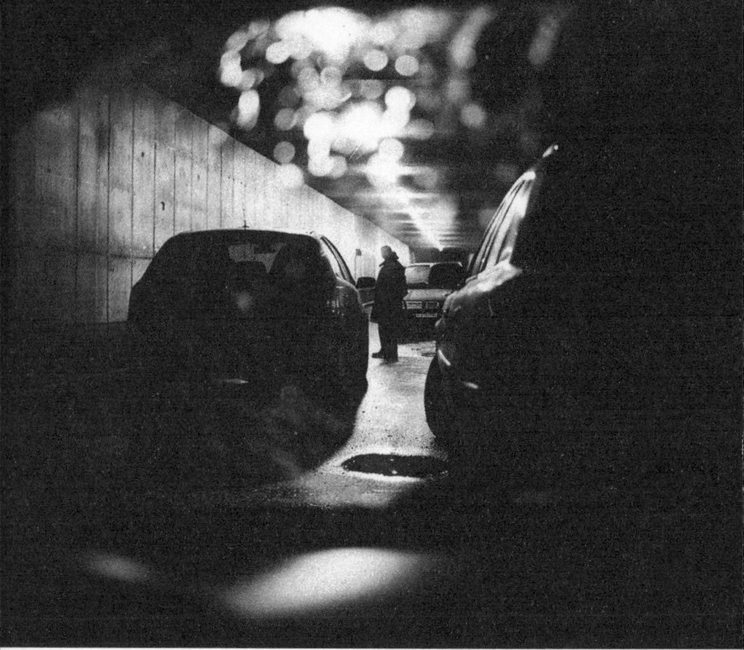

Even though getting in a car sound great, sometimes is way too obvious. Not only does bounce a lot, but the windows fog up make it hard to see if a guard is coming. I don't know... not my thing. I prefer it outdoors.

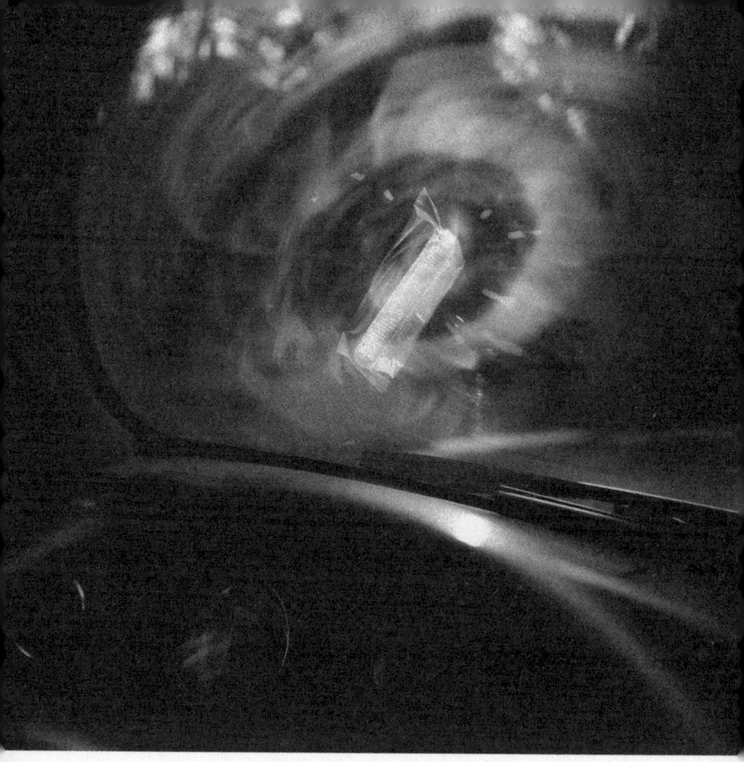

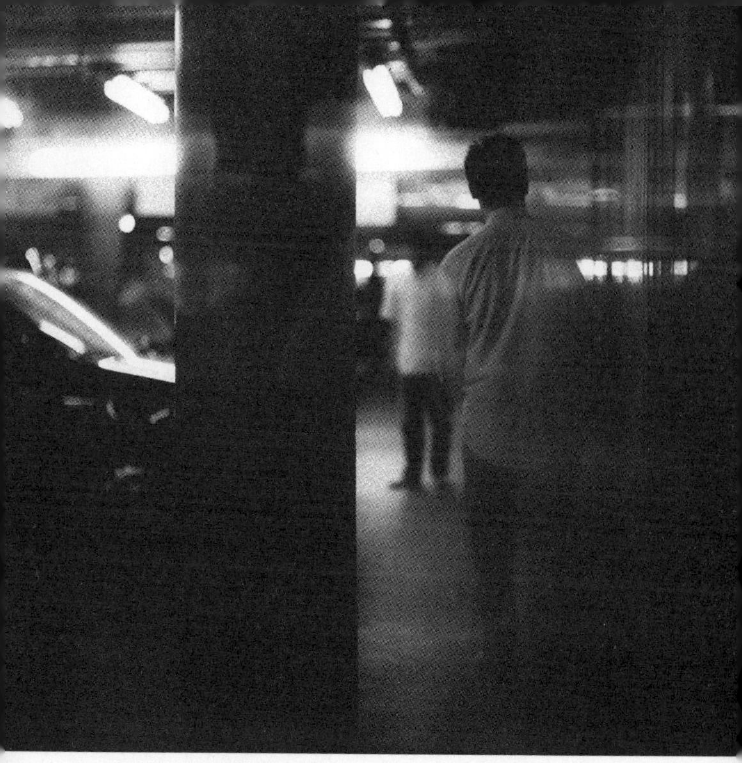

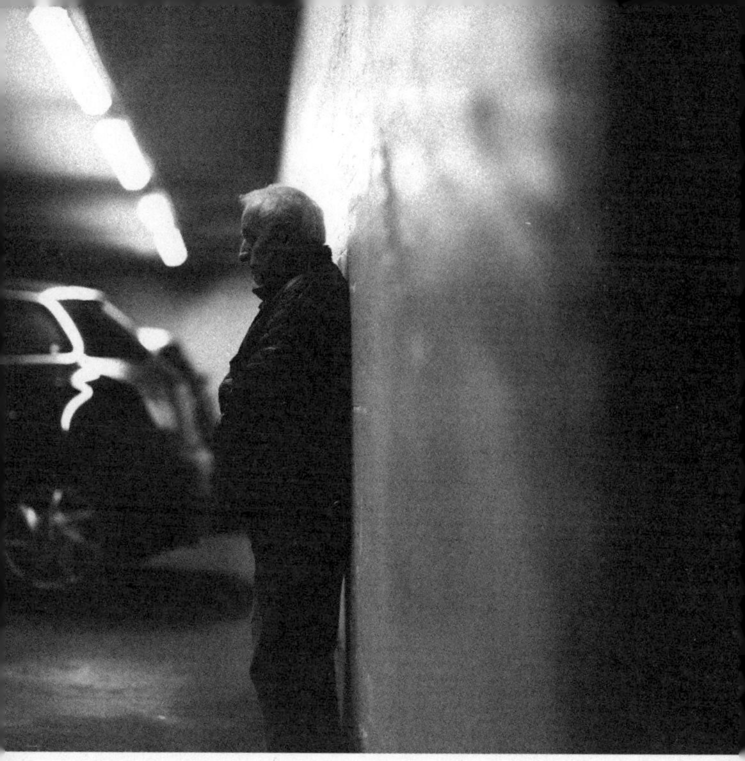

There is no doubt that these bathrooms were designed by a fag:

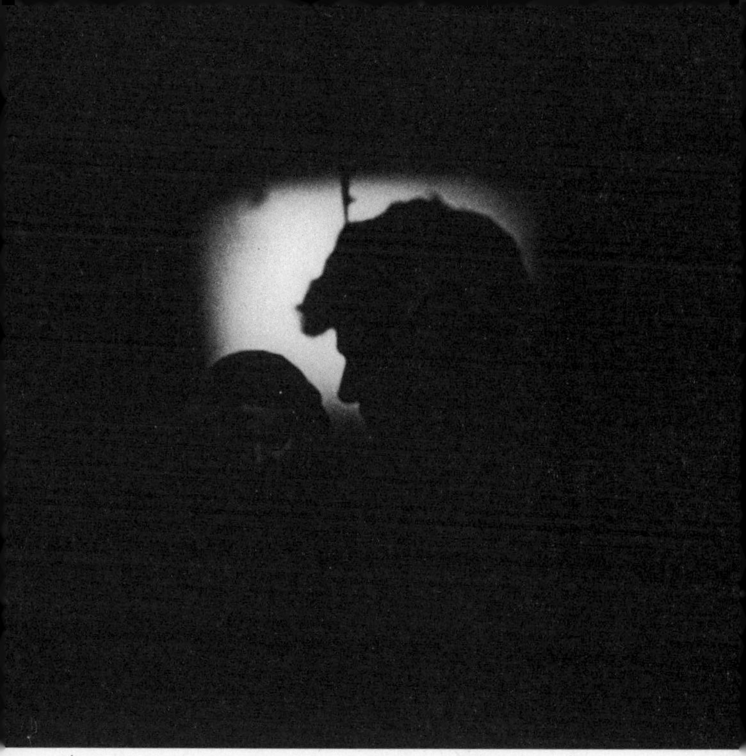

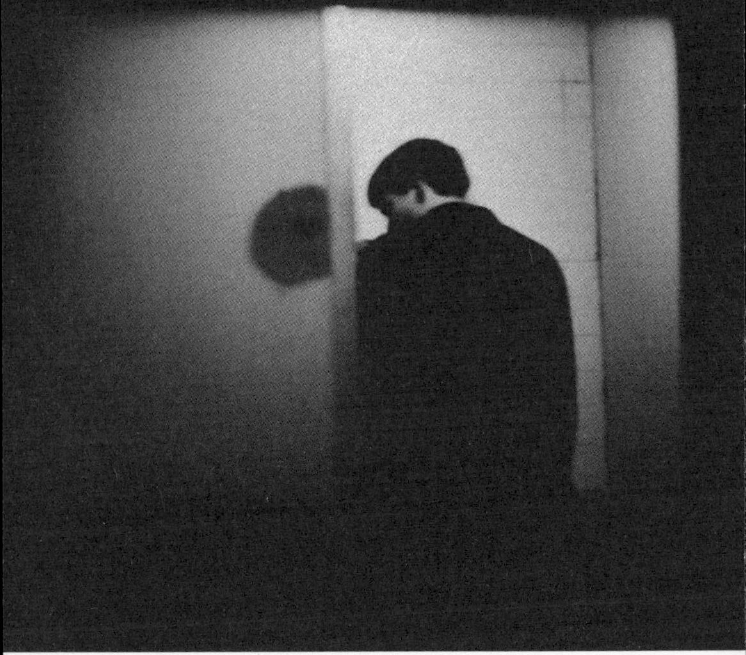

The door to the entrance squeaks when it opens (and it opens outward, giving you a bit more time if you're caught)

The stall doors go all the way to the floor. Great.

There's also a mirror above the sink directly in front of the stalls, making it easy to figure out if someone's only taking a leak without being obvious.

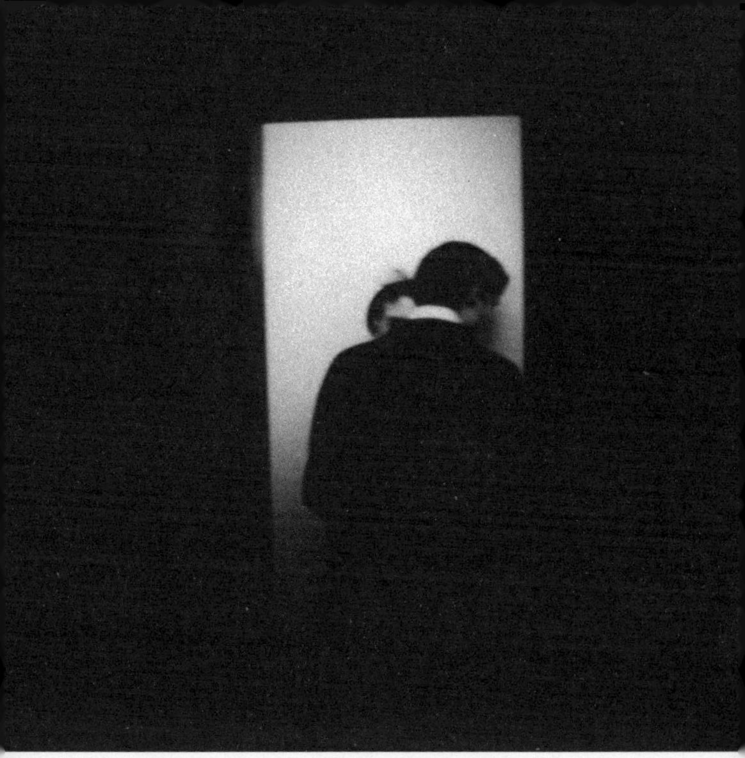

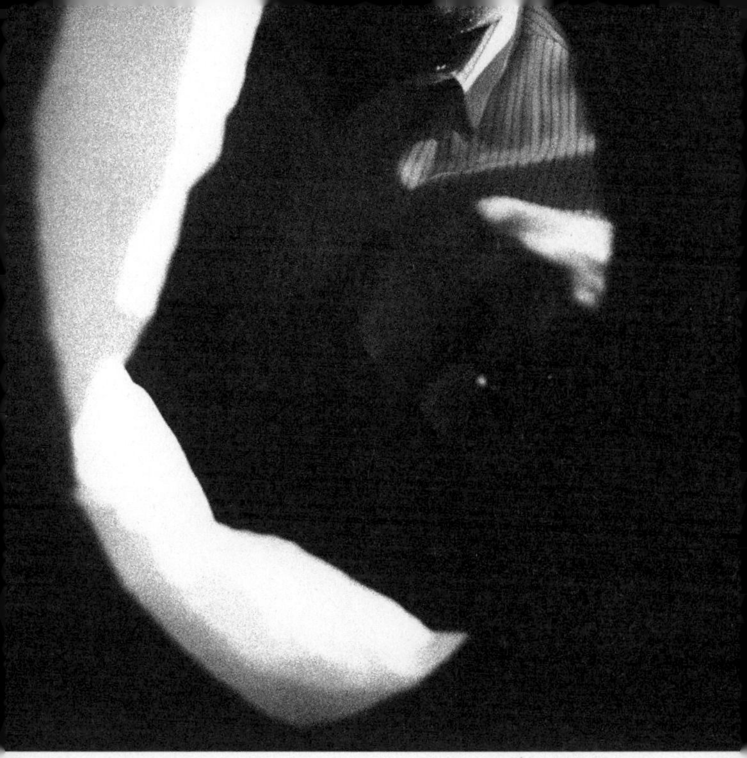

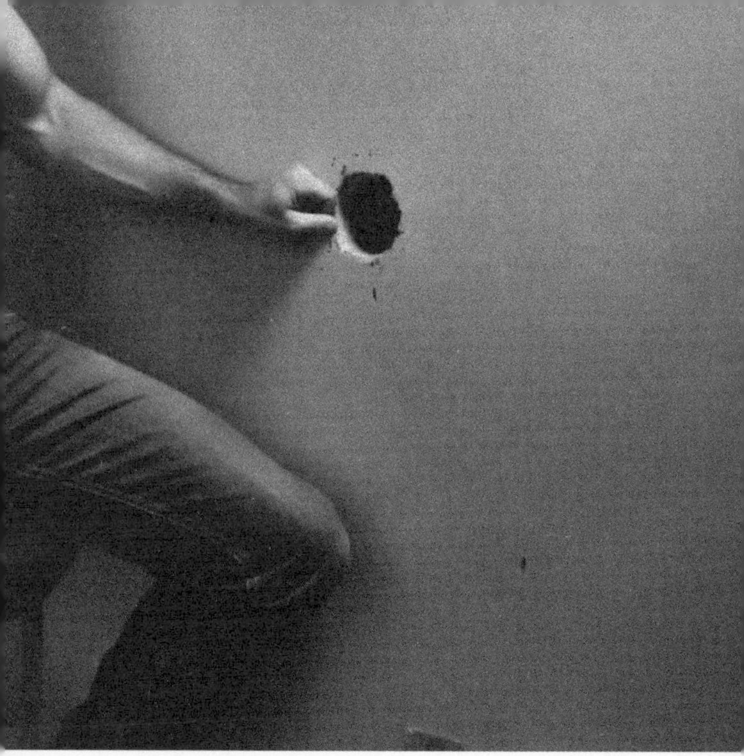

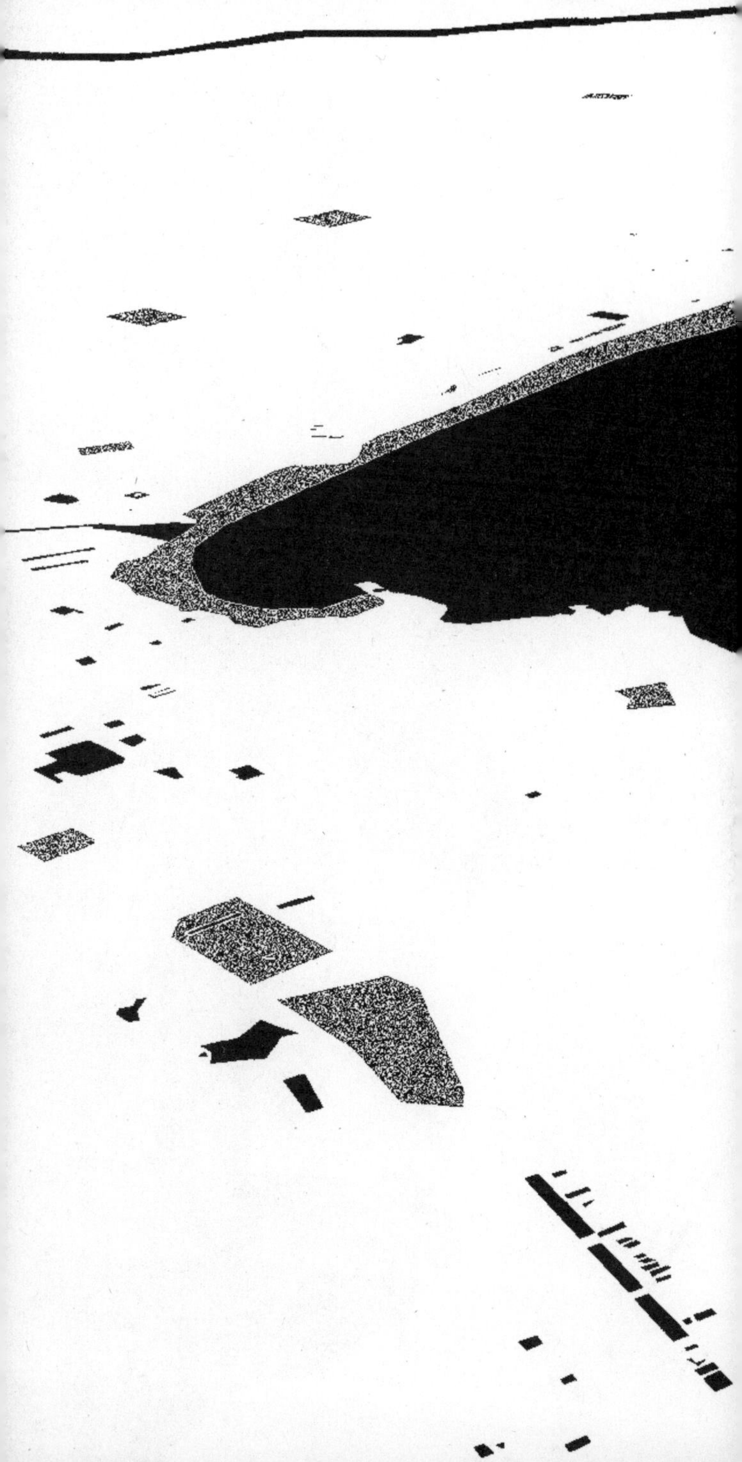

13. Love Beach Entrance

14. Abandoned House - Virgin's Grotto

15. Barefoot Hotel

16. Sand Dunes at Jasmine Beach

13. Love Beach Entrance

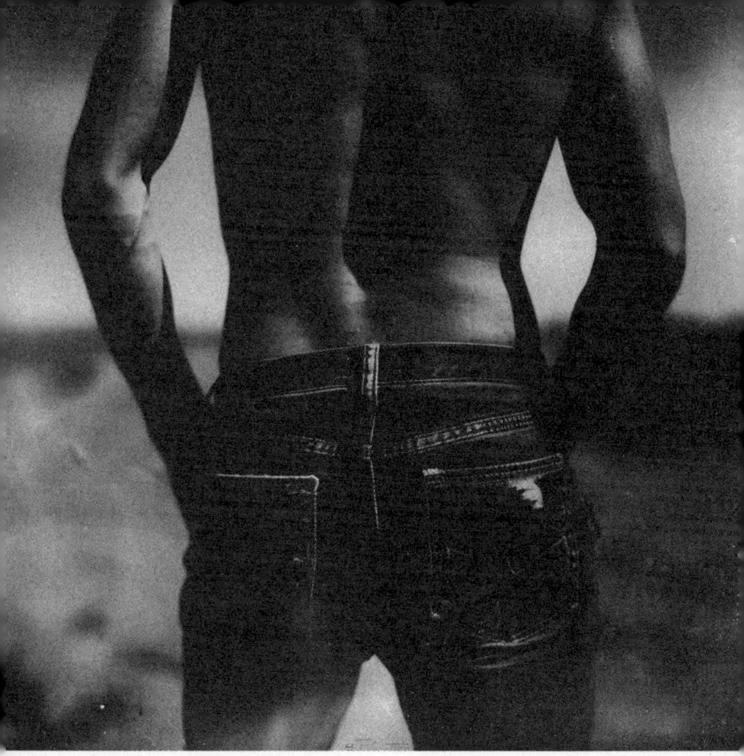

Summer months hit different.

You take the metro, then a 15-minute Uber. From there, you walk down until you reach a place we call 'Playa del Amor'.
During the day, it's the only nudist area in the city. At night — especially after 7 PM — it gets even better.

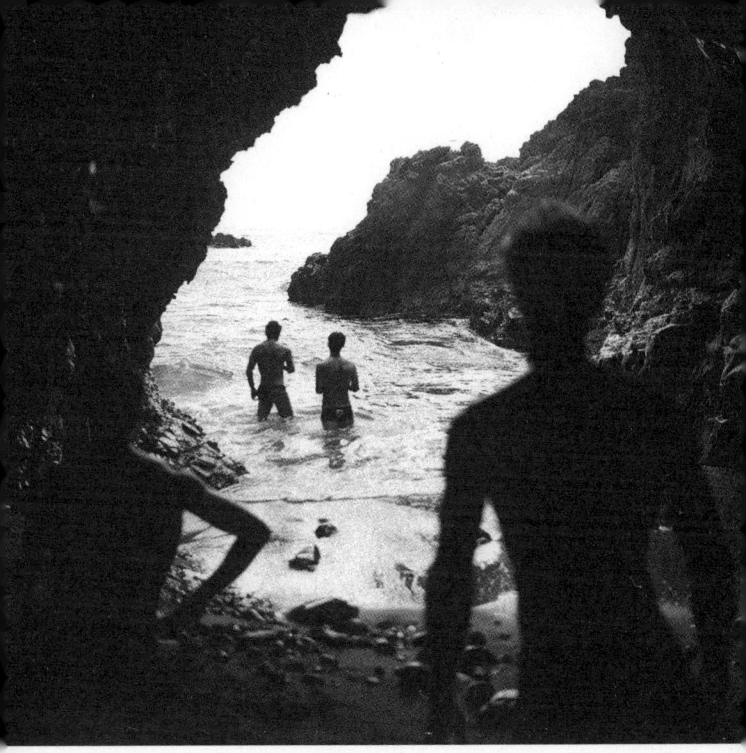

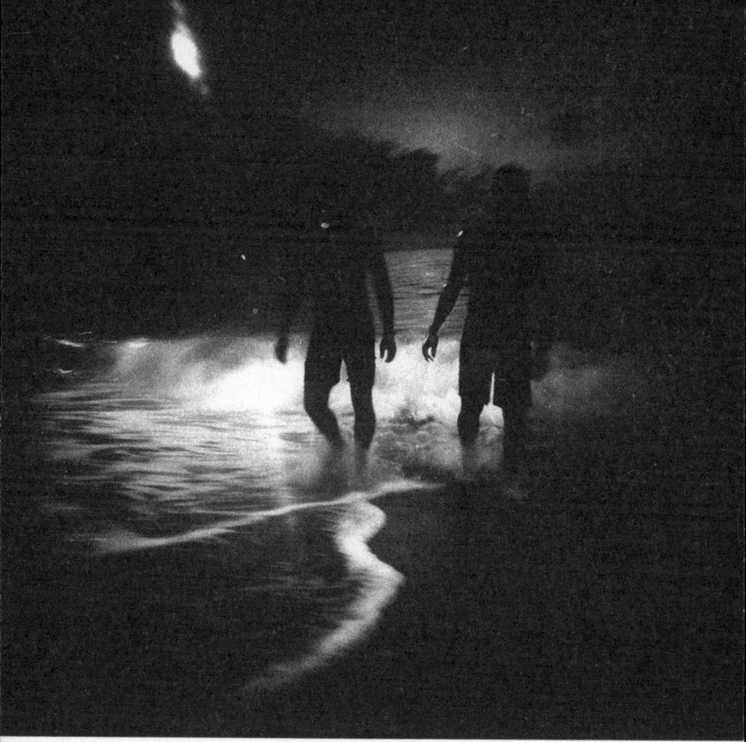

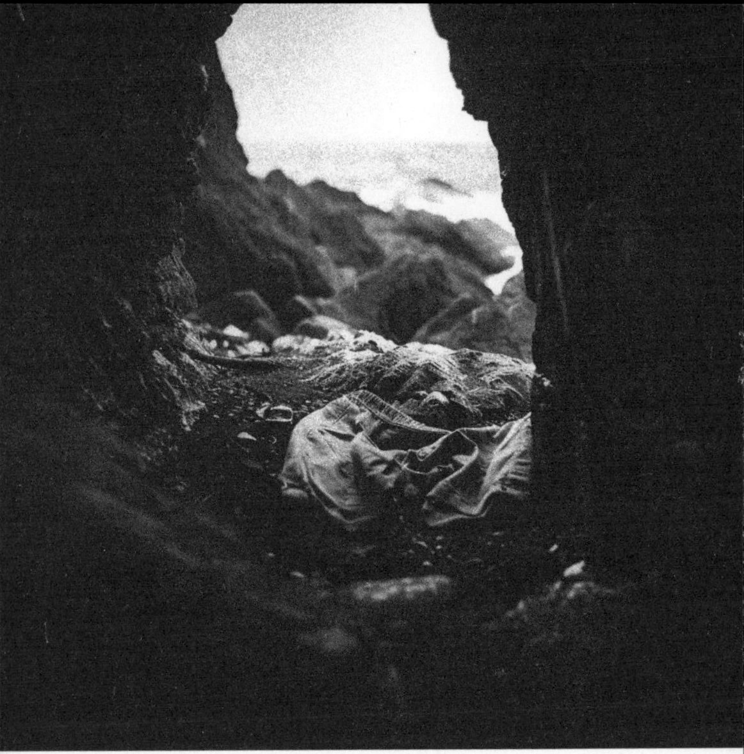

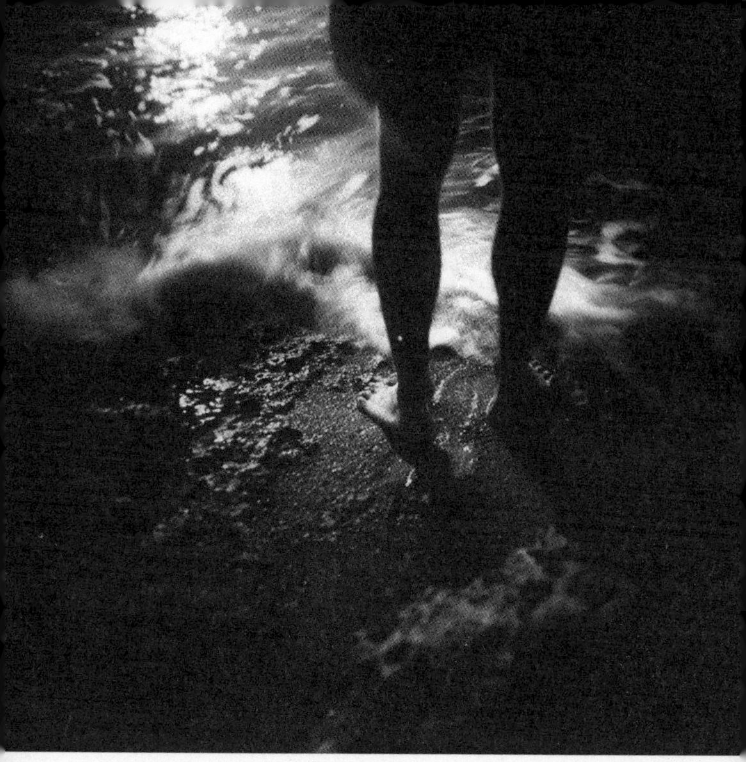

If you want a private place to fuck , then go a little further into the water and find a private spot amongst the rocks and cliffs.

Watch out during full moons; though it might seem romantic, the tide gets crazy high, making it tricky to get back. Apparently, a couple of guys drowned a few years back.

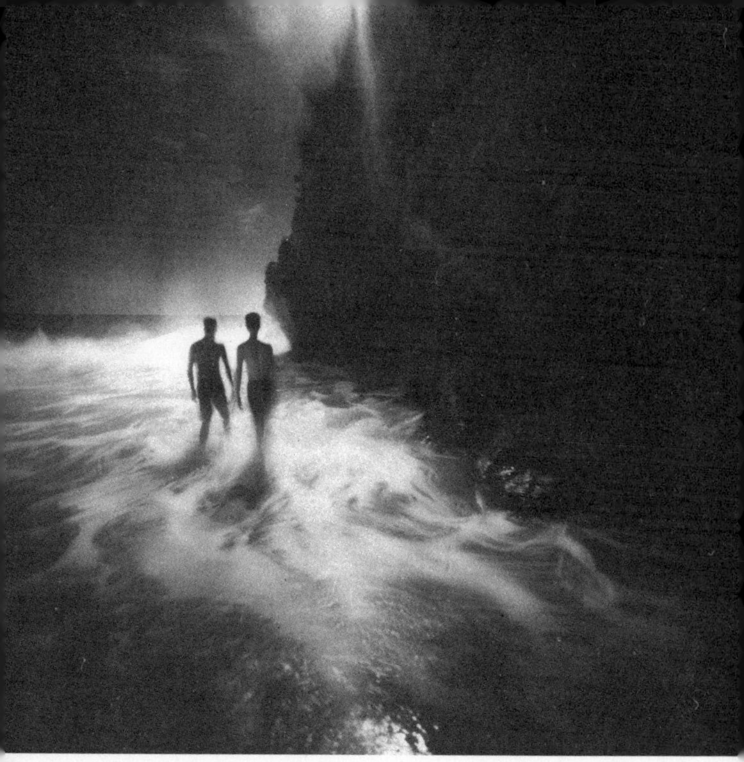

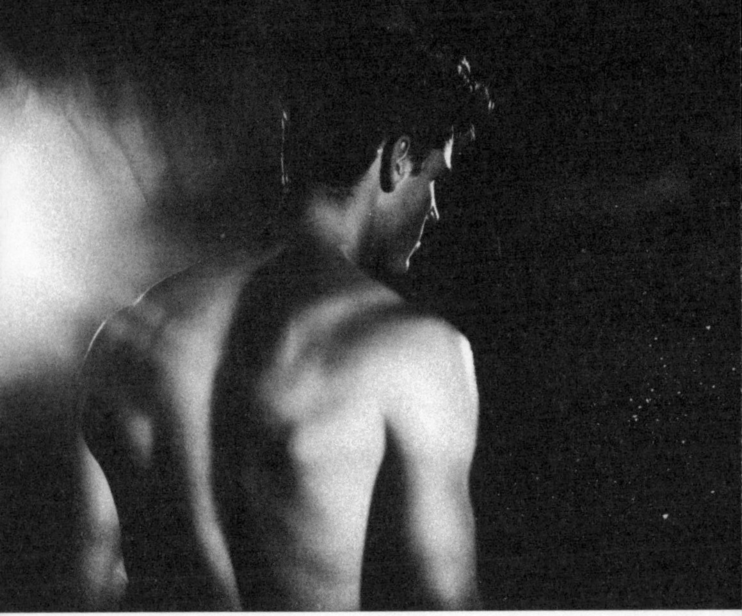

There's this cave that's pretty wild. Depending on the day (and the tide), it can be a condom graveyard. I've walked in and found more than 15 guys fucking in there. It's deep enough for daytime fun and definitely a hotspot at night. Smells like shit in there, but it gets the job done.

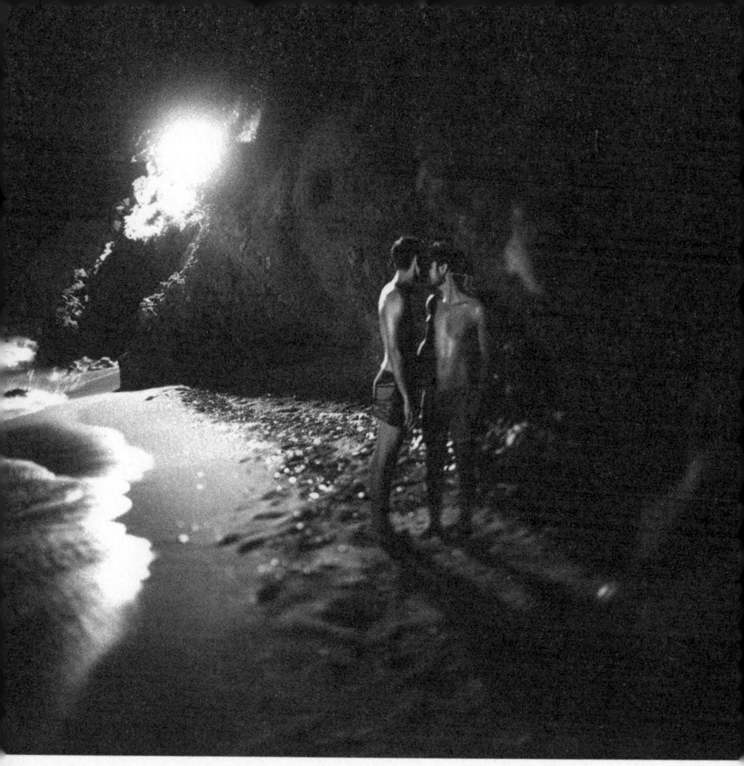

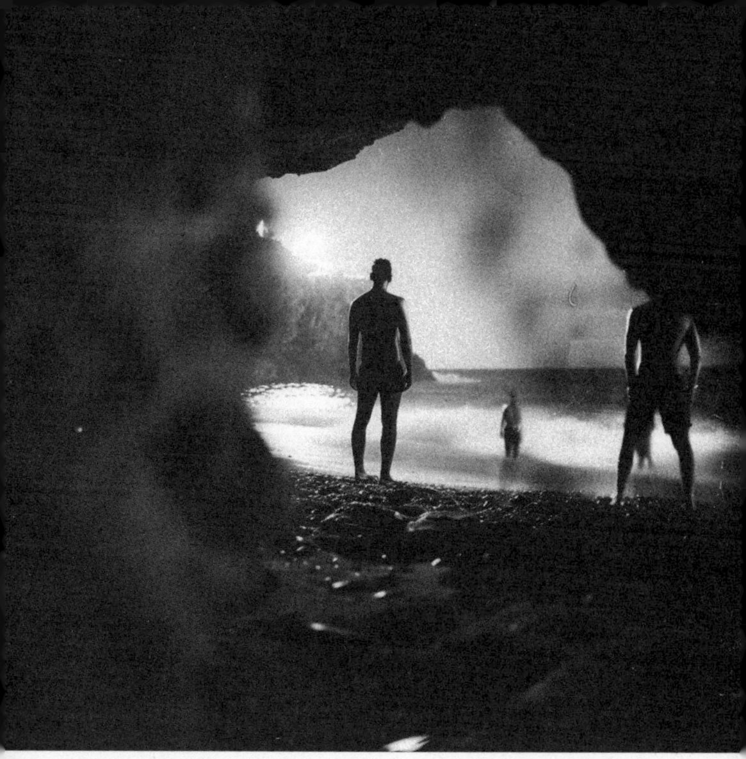

Beach = Patience.
Cruising always takes time, but especially here where people are doing all sorts of things, gay or not. It seems basic, but grabbing your bulge and making eye contact always does the trick.

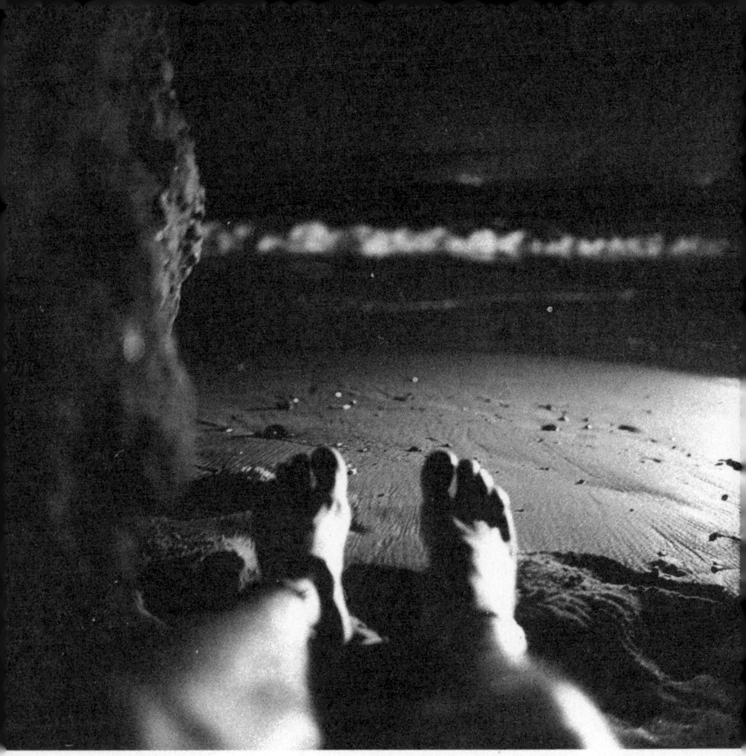

14. Abandoned House -Virgin's Grotto

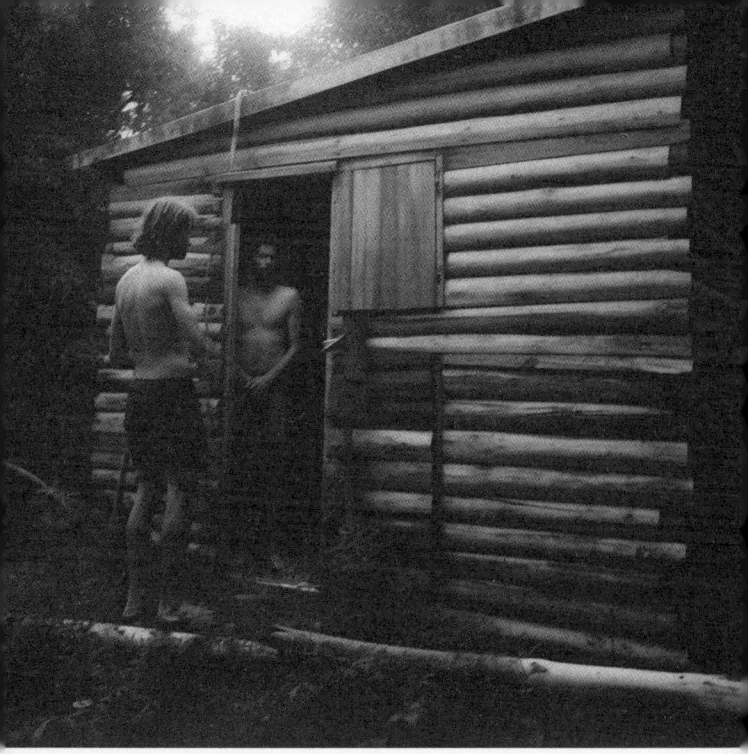

On the way to the Virgin's Grotto, there are some old storage cabins, that are now perfect for some action.

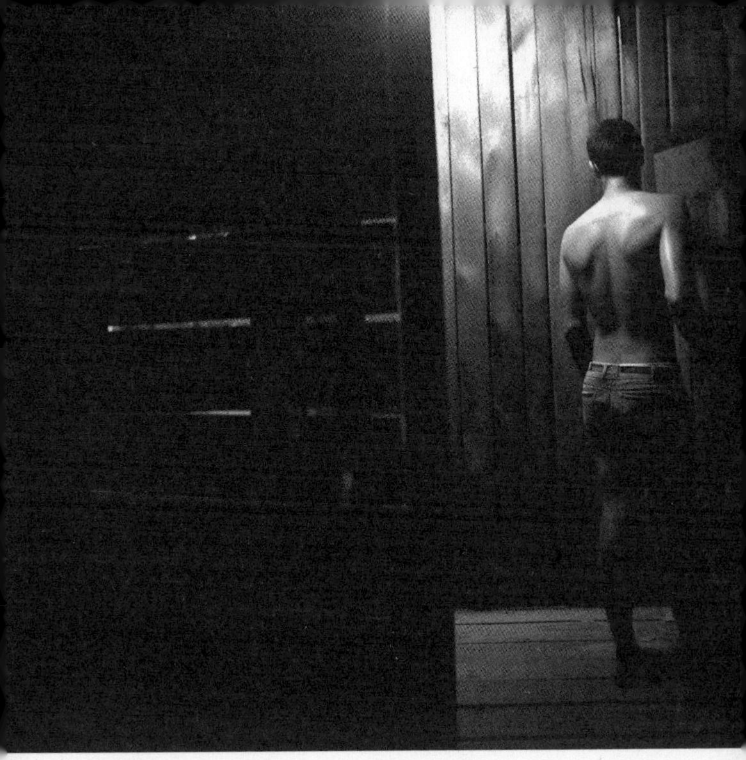

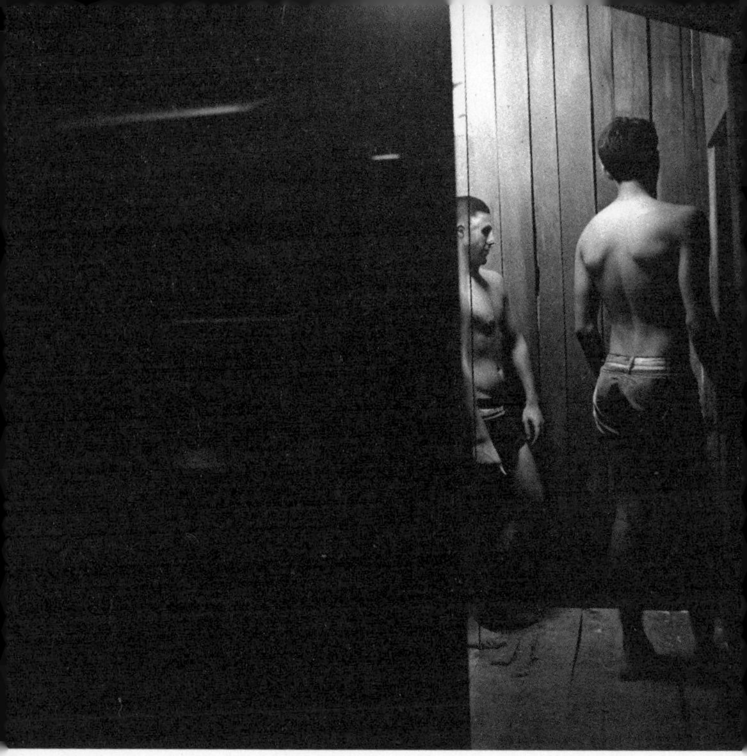

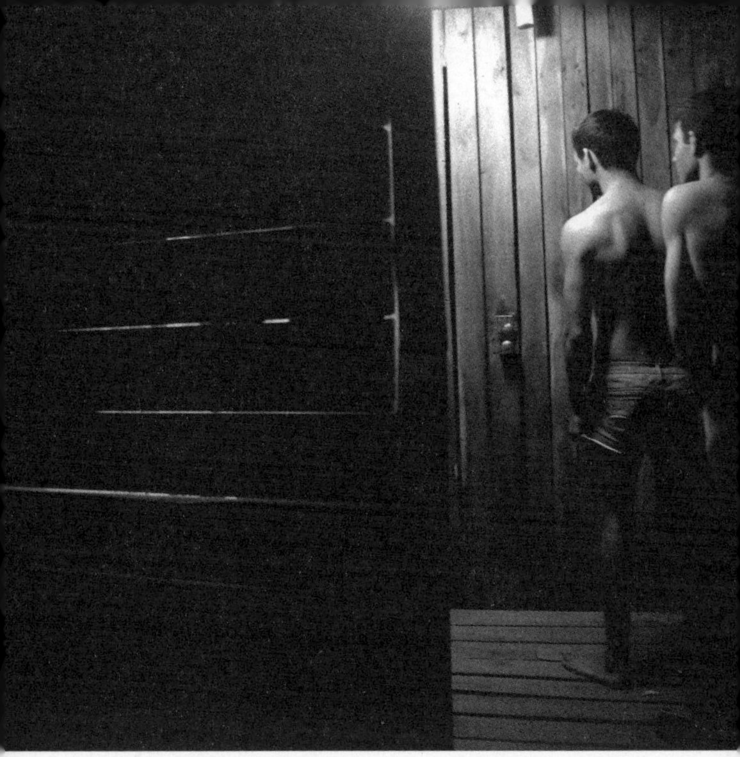

No one's just 'hanging out there'; it's all about picking someone up from the nudist beach, day or night, and heading to these cabins. Great for groups too, super chill, and you can hear if anyone's coming.

Nighttime back can be a maze; it's dark and easy to get lost.

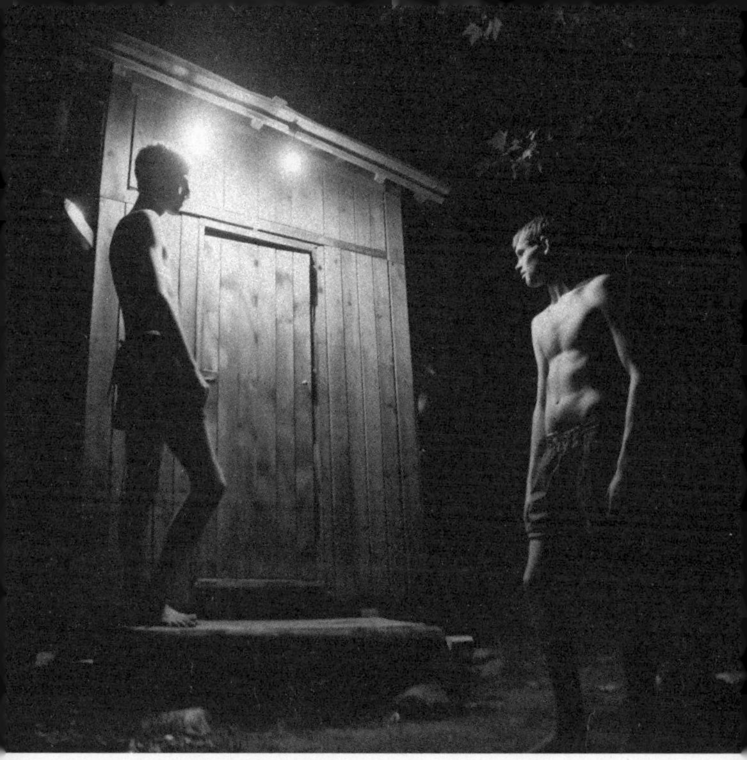

15. Barefoot Hotel

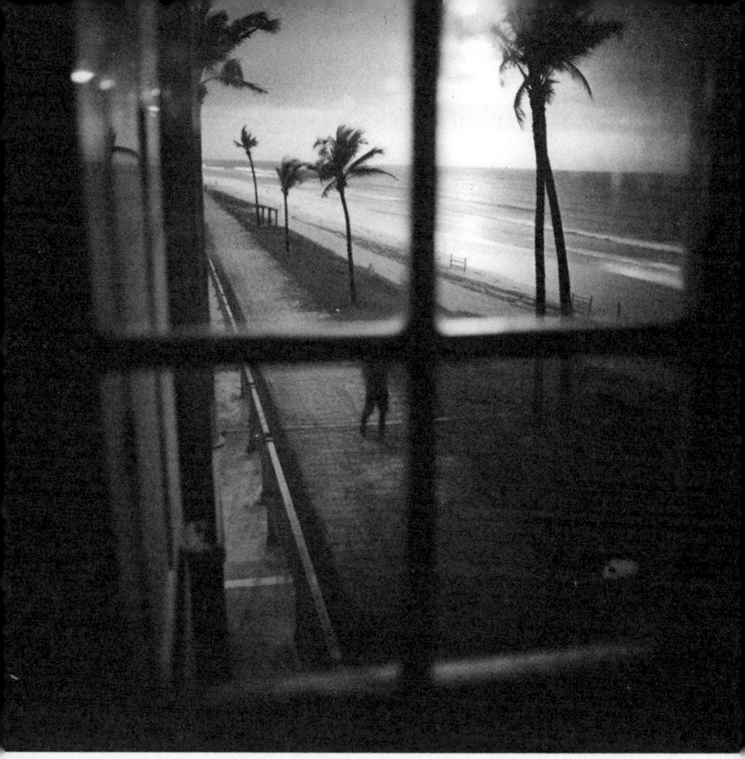

You can pay for a 'Day Pass' in Hotel Descalzo. That includes the pool, sauna, bar, etc.

Men-only place (99% gay of course)

Usually good tunes at the pool and a solid cruising spot.

Lots of foreigners too; I would suggest to snag one staying there and head up to his room.

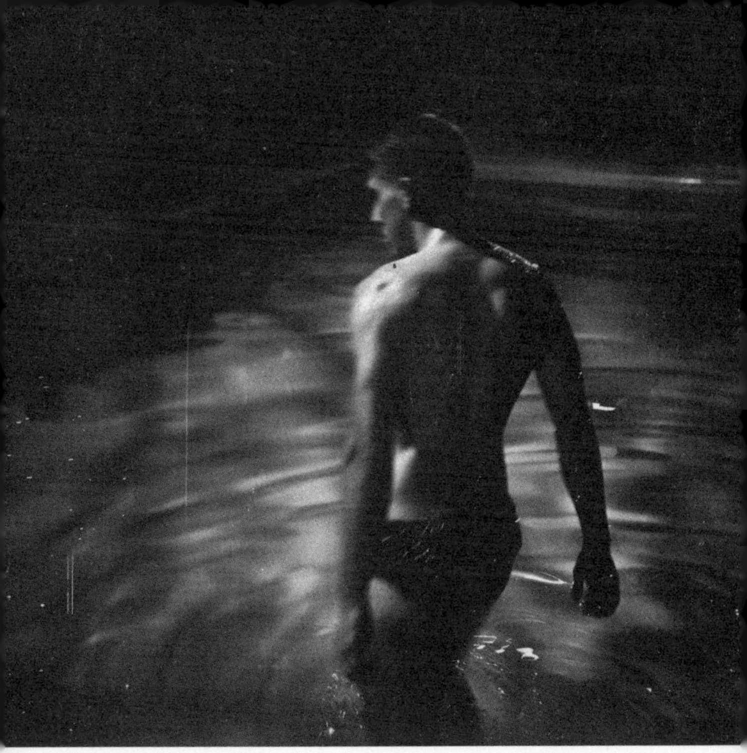

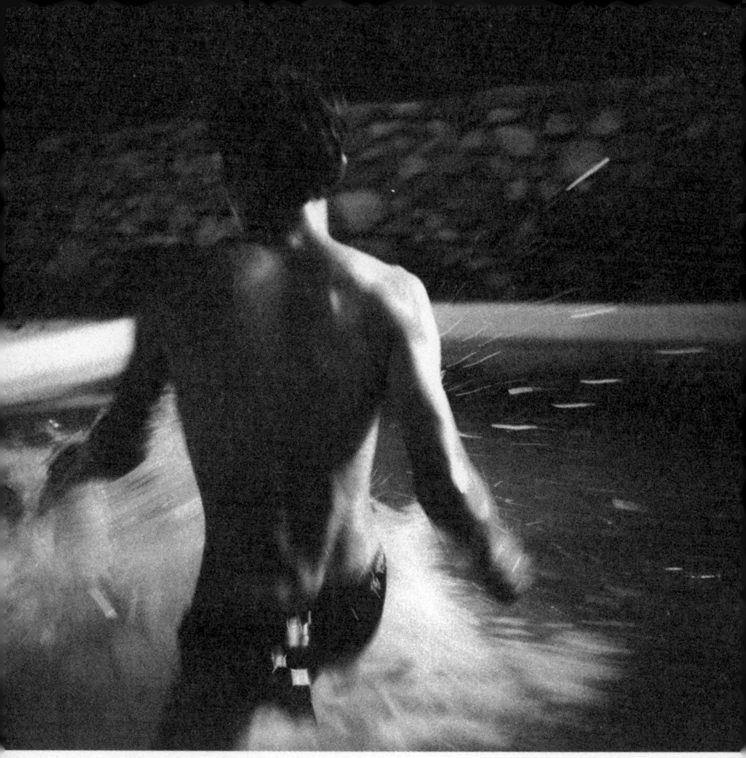

The bar's decent, nothing fancy, fair prices.

Last I knew, a hot bartender named 'Tato' was working there.

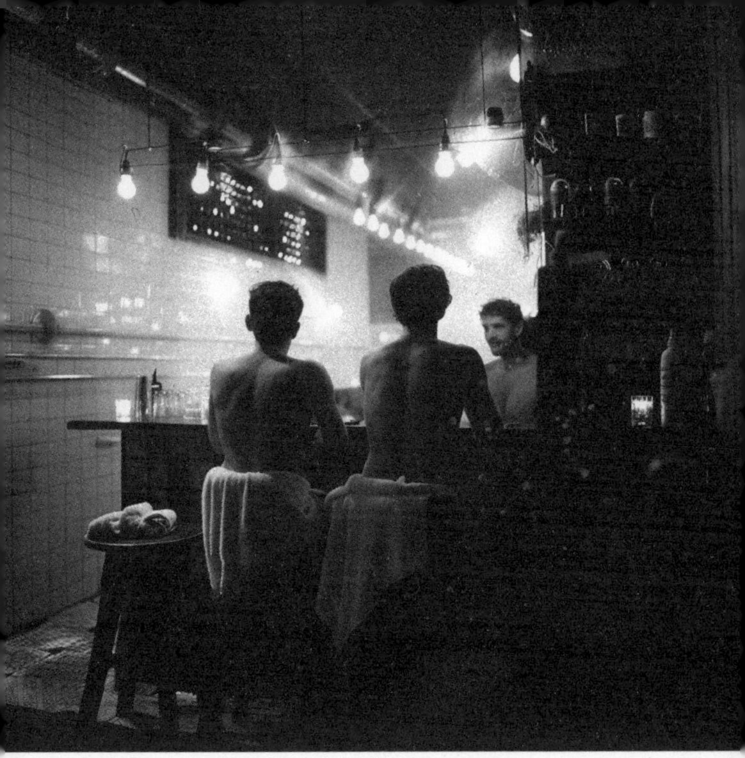

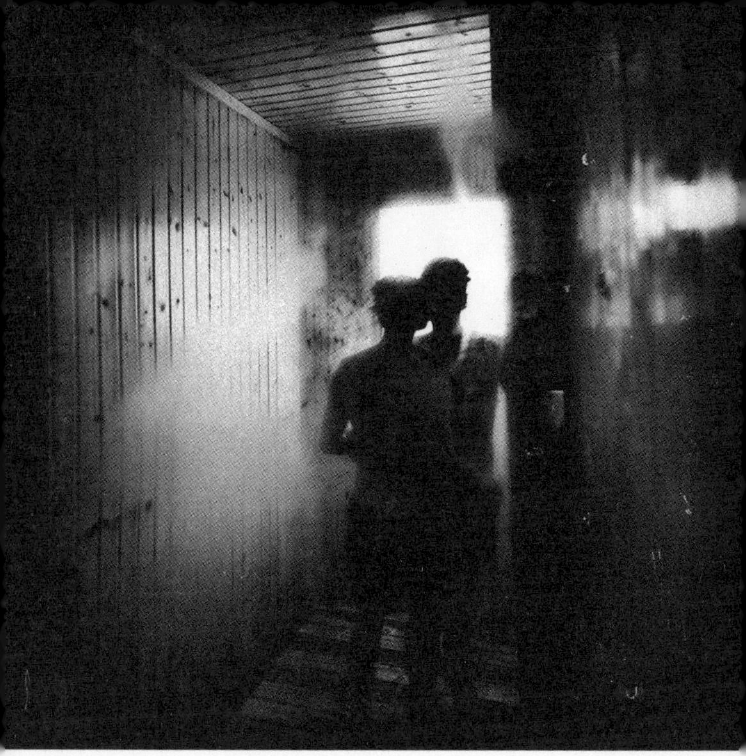

Entry's not cheap, but a day with sauna + pool + action— worths it.

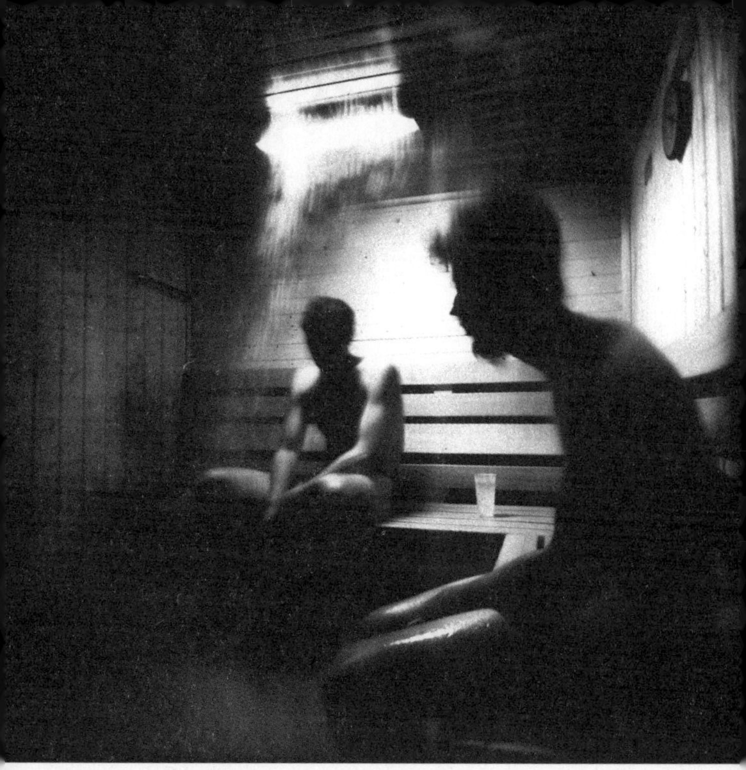

16. Sand Dunes at Jasmine Beach

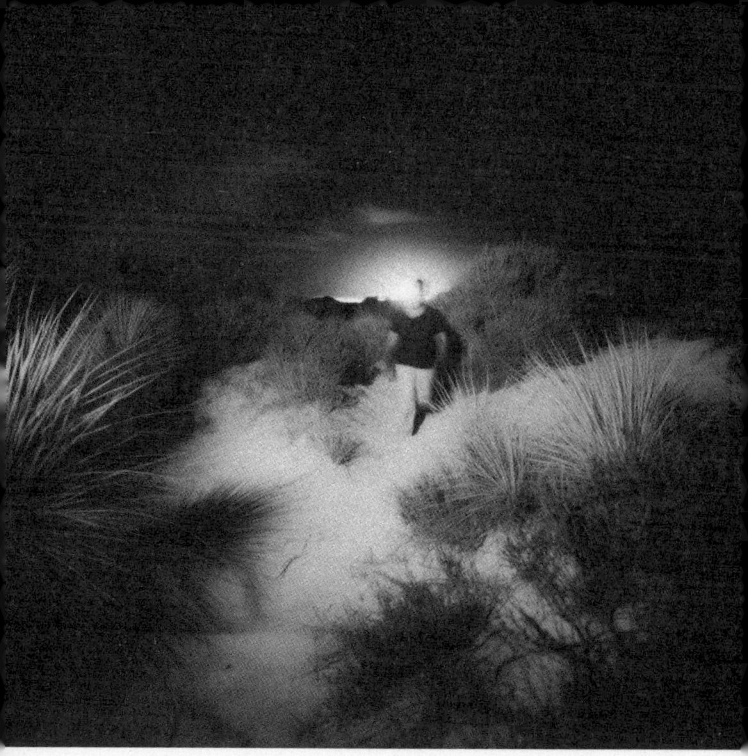

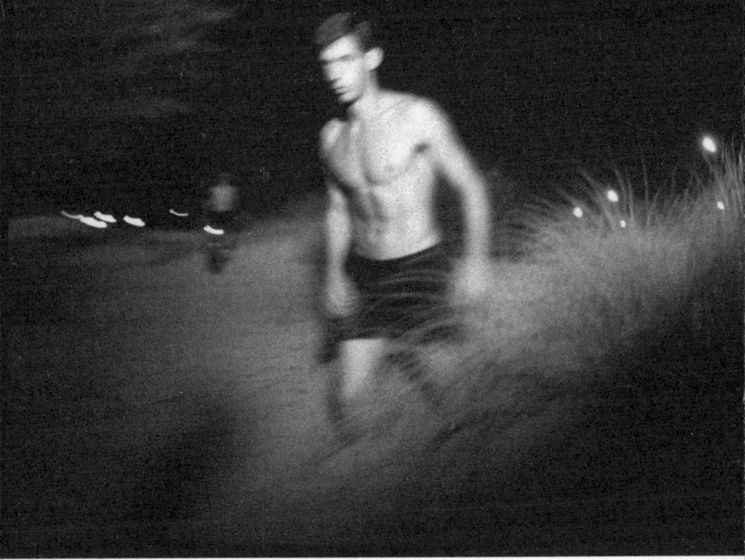

Along the beach near Punta Ángel, there's always someone around in the early hours. Horny young guys spill out of clubs, looking for someone to blow them.

Fucking on the sand isn't the most comfortable thing in the world. If that's your plan, I recommend going prepared with a mat and mosquito repellent. Mosquitoes can be a pain depending on the season.

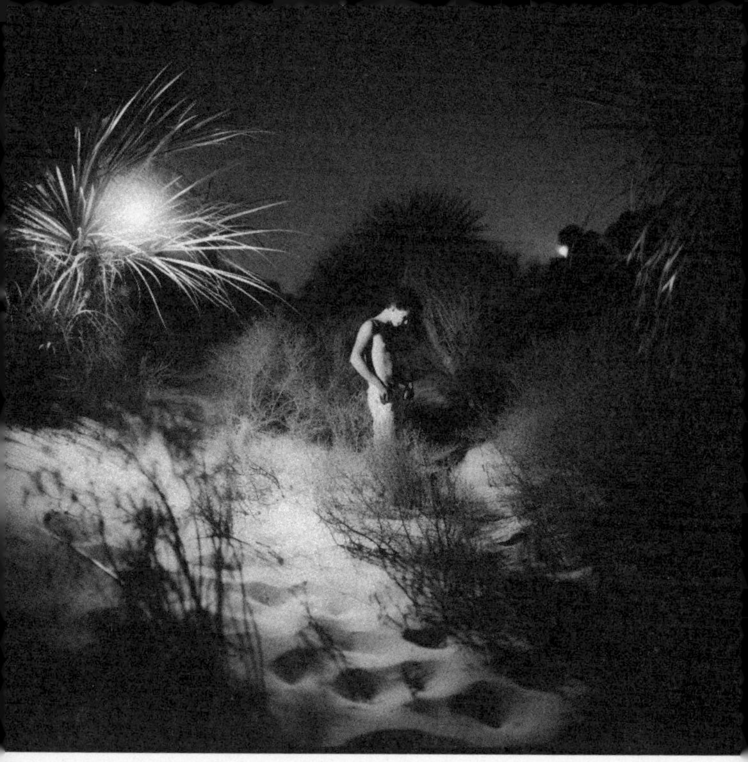

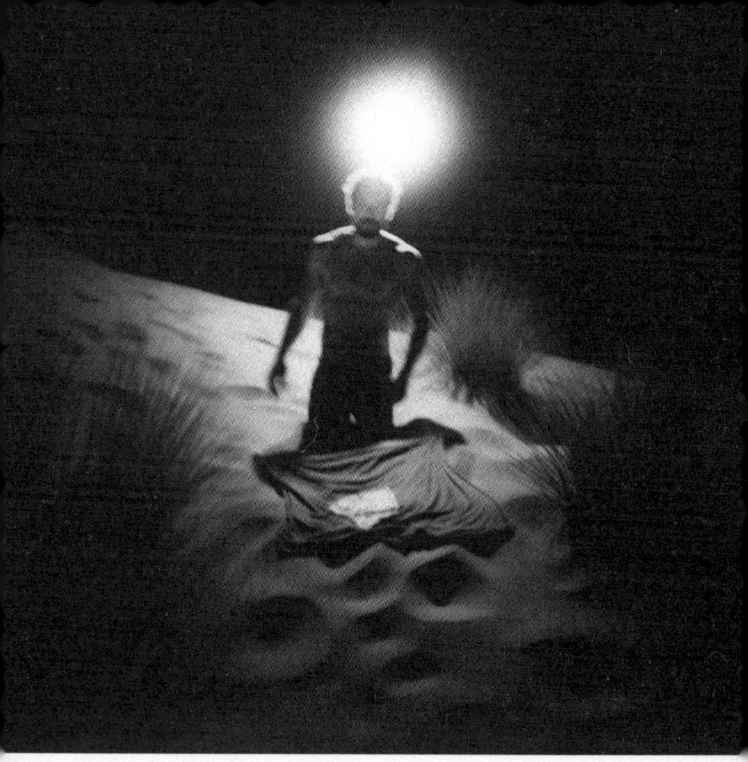

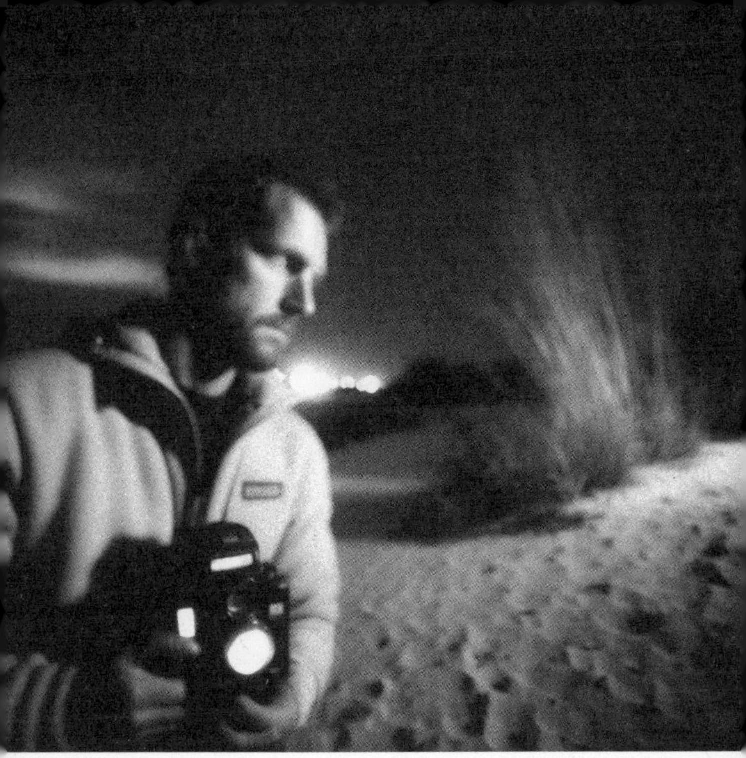

Set Margins' #47

ISBN 978-90-834993-5-2

By Franco Dupuy

Book Design: Furio + Santiago Bogani
Image editor: Franco Dupuy
Printer: Printon, Tallin, Estonia

Made possible by Franco Dupuy and
Set Margins' publications

First edition 2025, 1250 copies.
Second edition, February 2026, 2500 copies.

CRUISING IS ANONYMOUS

CRUISING IS FURTIVE

CRUISING IS DARK